KAUFMANN'S

LETITIA STUART SAVAGE

KAUFMANN'S

The Big Store in Pittsburgh

THE
History
PRESS

Published by The History Press
Charleston, SC
www.historypress.net

All images courtesy of Detre Library and Archives Division, Heinz History Center,
Pittsburgh, Pennsylvania.

First published 2016

Manufactured in the United States

ISBN 978.1.46711.990.0

Library of Congress Control Number: 2016944006

For my mother, who introduced us to Kaufmann's shopping and lunch at the Tic Toc.

CONTENTS

ACKNOWLEDGEMENTS

$\mathcal{A}$rchivists and volunteers at the Senator John Heinz History Center for help identifying and accessing the Kaufmann's Department Store manuscripts and photographs: thank you for scanning to meet our deadlines and for working out of borrowed space on an April Saturday rather than closing the archives during a history center conference.

Those "Kaufmannites" who donated materials now in the Heinz History Center archives.

The *Pittsburgh Post-Gazette* for scanning its extensive newspaper archives and making them available online. This archive provided more than one hundred years of advertisements and news articles on Kaufmann's, including material that wasn't available elsewhere. For those who would like to "shop" the stores of the past, this archive can provide hours of entertainment.

Northland Public Library, whose librarians and volunteers provided interlibrary loan services.

All of the people who shared their memories of the store over the years with the press and online. Each memory is a piece of history.

My husband and research associate, William Ebner, who persisted with Kaufmann's material when he would rather have been reading Fort Pitt's 1763 daybook.

MEET ME UNDER THE CLOCK

*W*hen Macy's decided to close its Downtown Pittsburgh store in September 2015, the public responded with a flood of shared memories. While the historic Kaufmann's building would remain, it would no longer house a department store. There would be no more thumbprint cookies from the Arcade Bakery and no more lunches at the Tic Toc Restaurant. But the iconic clock would survive.

As Pittsburghers mourned the final demise of the store, they celebrated the clock. For almost a century, meeting under the clock had been a city tradition. For more than a century, the clock was a symbol of Kaufmann's.

The first Kaufmann's clock with four faces stood on a pedestal on the corner in front of the store. A sign on the pedestal encouraged, "Meet Me Under the Clock." Built in 1884, it was removed when the store was expanded in 1912. There was an immediate public outcry. Henry Kaufmann ordered an ornate brass clock from the Coldwell Clock Company in New York and had it installed on the building in 1913.

By World War II, the clock had become the recognized symbol of the store, and its role as a meeting place was celebrated in *Yank* magazine. In December 1981, it and the Kaufmann's building were granted landmark status by the Pittsburgh History and Landmarks Foundation.

Six years later, the clock disappeared again, and the public noticed. But the clock was gone for all the right reasons. Kaufmann's, as part of a major renovation, had sent it for restoration. It took three days to carefully remove and label one hundred pieces of the ornate metalwork. Three teams of

The original Kaufmann's clock was four-faced and stood on a pedestal at the corner of Fifth Avenue and Smithfield Street. When it was removed during the store's 1912 expansion, there was such public outcry that Henry Kaufmann ordered a new clock, which was installed on the store building.

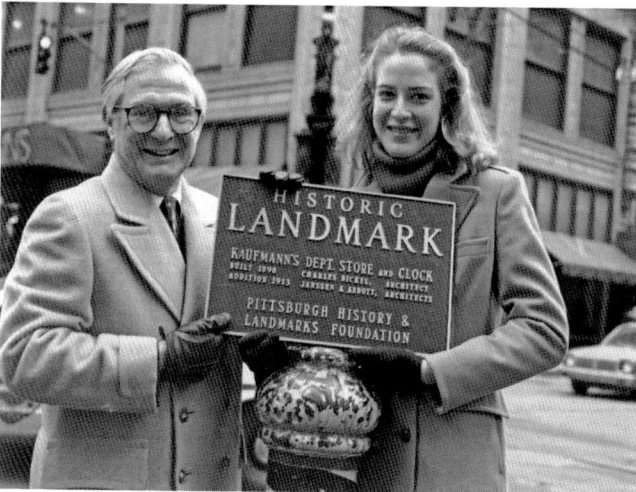

In 1981, Kaufmann's building and iconic clock received landmark status from the Pittsburgh History and Landmarks Foundation. The plaque remained on the building after Kaufmann's became a Macy's store in 2005.

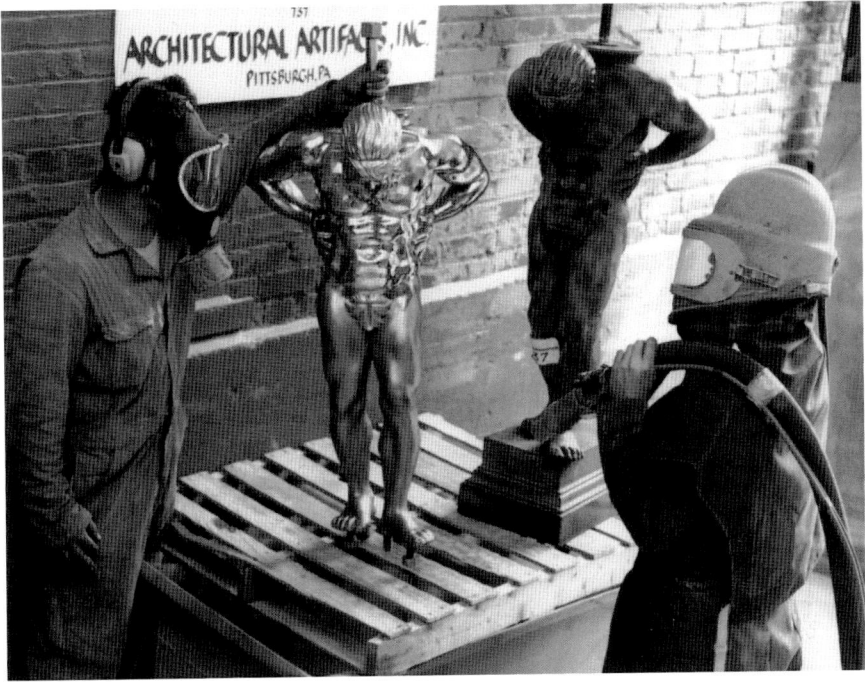

The clock was removed and restored during the spring and summer of 1987. Local specialists recast missing and damaged pieces and sandblasted and polished the ornate figures.

fifteen local specialists worked for ten weeks to clean, polish and restore the 2,500-pound brass clock. They made new molds for missing and damaged parts and cast replacements. They installed a new, dual-drive movement. The restored clock was unveiled on Light Up Night in November 1987, just in time for holiday meetups.

Although the beloved store is gone, the new owner of the Kaufmann's building, CORE Realty, has committed to retaining the clock as it converts the building to mixed commercial/residential use. But the iconic store was always more than the clock out front.

Chapter 1

A NEW "COMMERCIAL BABY"

When Jacob Kaufmann immigrated to the United States in 1868 from Viernheim, Germany, he didn't find work in the sweatshops of New York, like so many other immigrant tailors did. Instead, he headed for western Pennsylvania, where he invested his limited funds in merchandise and became an itinerant peddler. Carrying his goods on his back, he traveled on foot through the rural counties outside Pittsburgh. He saved his profits and was soon able to ask his brother Isaac to join him. His goal was to set up a tailor shop.

On May 25, 1871, a local newspaper on Pittsburgh's South Side carried a small advertisement announcing the "birth of a commercial baby" at 1916 Carson Street. Jacob and Isaac had opened a small clothing shop called J. Kaufmann and Brother. The South Side had no clothing store, and the construction of a large Jones and Laughlin steel mill nearby was bringing working men to the neighborhood. In addition to tailoring, the brothers carried a small stock of men's ready-to-wear clothing. The store offered suits cut from "the latest Philadelphia and New York patterns," which required considerable skill. The tiny space, 476 square feet, was dominated by a large cutting table and crowded with bolts of fabric. The brothers also added a couch where they slept after working late into the night. The next year, they moved into a bigger space at 1932 Carson Street.

Isaac and Jacob had inherited considerable business sense from their father, Abraham Kaufmann, who was a successful cattle dealer. He advised them, "Sell to others as you would buy for yourself." His advice became the

Brothers Isaac and Jacob Kaufmann founded the store in 1871 with $1,500 in cash that Jacob had saved while working as an itinerant peddler. Isaac later remembered their early struggle; the founding decade of the store coincided with a financial depression that lasted from 1873 until 1879.

guiding principles of the business: "Good merchants make small profits and many sales…Deal fairly and be patient and in time dishonest competitors will crowd your store with customers."

Although the brothers later wrote that those first years in business were on a "slender footing which could not be risked by so much as the loss of a single customer," they recorded sales of $21,585 during their first year of business.

In 1872, fourteen-year-old Morris joined his brothers. As the youngest of the three, he slept on the second floor to discourage burglars and remembered getting up at night to empty buckets that collected water from the leaking roof. Morris tied a string to his toe and ran it out the window at the front of the store. If he overslept, a sharp tug would wake him.

Kaufmann and Brothers was soon a popular and profitable store. Shoppers from Pittsburgh crossed the river to buy clothing. In 1874, the brothers opened a branch store at Federal and South Diamond Street in Allegheny (now the North Side) and moved the South Side store to larger quarters at 634 Market Street. In 1876, twelve-year-old Henry arrived from Germany.

By 1877, business was brisk enough to allow the brothers to close both the South Side and North Side shops and move to 83 Smithfield Street and Diamond Street (now Forbes Avenue) in Downtown Pittsburgh. "Kaufmann's Cheapest Corner," as they called their enterprise in 1879, had expanded to four stories and was ready to conquer city retail. The top two floors were rented as office space for additional income, and the brothers hired three employees to help them make and sell clothing.

9522 Kaufmann's - "The Big Store" - Pittsburg.

Kaufmann's downtown store in 1912. A Goddess of Liberty was mounted on top of the corner tower, her torch fueled by natural gas. At the time, the store was known as the "Grand Depot."

After its move downtown but before the 1912 expansion, Kaufmann's occupied a variety of neighboring buildings. This image from the 1880s shows the original store on the corner with the adjacent buildings that it would later purchase for expansion.

The Kaufmann brothers had advertised very little in the local newspapers, but on October 25, 1880, they placed their first ad in the *Pittsburgh Daily Post*. Now calling itself J. Kaufmann and Brothers, the store used large headlines and dramatic language to call attention to its lists of ready-made clothing for men and boys that fall. Then it did something extraordinary: it listed its prices. Traditional dry goods stores didn't list prices. Prices varied depending on what the owners felt customers would pay. An experienced clerk would size up customers, and haggling was common. The Kaufmann brothers believed that everyone should pay the same price and used a "one price to all" strategy to differentiate themselves. Cards on merchandise displayed that price. The store also invited customers in to browse, another revolutionary retail concept.

The brothers summarized their business philosophy in their *Fashion Journal*, an early catalogue for mail-order customers:

> *In publishing this Journal we...desire to place ourselves...before the community, showing our methods of trading, which are so open that all can see their fairness. There is only ONE PRICE for each article and that is plainly marked upon it. No more nor less is asked or taken. No faults are*

concealed nor misrepresentation allowed. This system is a protection to every customer and does equal justice to all. It insures to the distant customer, who sends his order by mail, the same goods, process and advantages as our city trade get…We are positively the only retailers in the City of Pittsburgh, who manufacture their own Clothing and sell to the consumer with but One profit…The only Clothing sold by us, and which is not manufactured by ourselves, is such that we may accidentally have the opportunity to buy at an enormous sacrifice from overstocked or financially embarrassed manufacturers.

To emphasize their selling philosophy, they called their store "Kaufmanns 5 PerCent Profit Mammoth Clothing Emporium." Their ads stated, "We guarantee a savings of from 20 to 33 per cent on any article bought from us. Our fair dealing and one price to all. Money cheerfully refunded."

By the early 1880s, their business philosophy was paying off, and they had seventy-five employees. By 1881, Kaufmann's was advertising regularly in the *Pittsburgh Daily Post*. The brothers often bought lots of merchandise from failing retailers and offered the goods at huge sales. "We made four grand purchases, aggregating over $300,000 of Men's, Boy's and Children's Clothing, Hats and Gents' Furnishing Goods," an ad declared.

Early ads relied on colorful language, bold headlines and a variety of typefaces and sizes. Graphics were added later and were often drawings of individual sales items.

To attract attention, the ads used banner headlines and breathless language. "Can you afford," the store asked, "to dress your boys and pay for a suit for one that will clothe two or three? Can you afford to buy a Suit for yourself and pay almost twice its value? Can you afford to buy a Hat or article of Furnishing Goods and pay from 25 to 50 percent more than the same article can be bought of us?" "If you want," the headline screamed, "to be astonished, if you want to be gratified with Genuine Bargains, if you want to be entertained, instructed, pleased, and profited all at once, you must visit us."

The ads also attracted shoppers with price and selection: "Kaufmann's Cheapest Corner the Largest Clothing House in Western PA" and "Pittsburgh's Mammoth Clothing House." Most of them included long lists of the merchandise available and, by the end of the 1880s, included illustrations of fashionable gentlemen. At the bottom

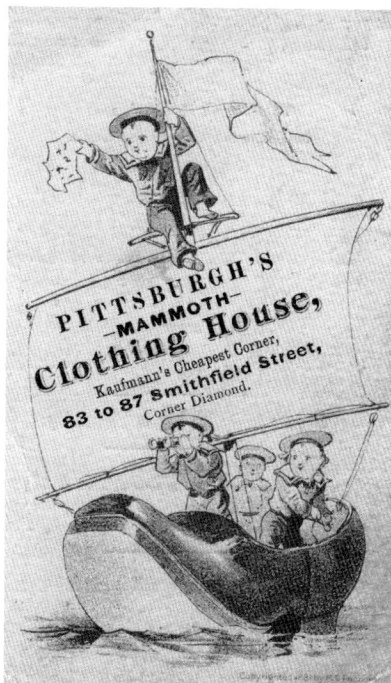

Like many stores, Kaufmann's used small cards with pictures on one side and advertising on the other to promote the store. This card for "Pittsburgh's Mammoth Clothing House" reminded shoppers that it carried clothing for boys.

of many ads, readers from outside the city were reminded that they could send for Kaufmann's free *Fashion Journal*, which included instructions so that buyers could enclose their measurements and have their purchases shipped to anywhere in the country.

In the early years of the store, the brothers advertised most heavily in the spring and in the fall, when they changed stock for the new seasons. The new merchandise would be introduced to the public during grand openings that often featured special events. An advertisement on March 17, 1884, for the spring opening advised that the store had become a "Grand Floral Temple" and that the opening on March 20 and 21 would include afternoon "Ladies' Receptions" and a "Grand Concert" from 7:30 p.m. to 10:00 p.m. For the fall opening late in September 1884, the store would once again feature flowers, as well as an "Automatic Window Display" and a "Unique Parisienne Perfume Fountain." A year later, the fall opening had an

Early department stores did not set fixed prices for merchandise. Clerks would vary prices depending on their assessment of what customers were willing to pay. Kaufmann's charged everyone the same "one price," which was neatly printed on cards. "Our motto—fair dealing—one price to all."

Oriental theme with stuffed birds, hanging flower baskets, balloons, fans, parasols and lanterns. Grand openings lasted at least until the spring of 1887, and the store started to sell some non-clothing items like lap desks and toilet sets.

Until the mid-1880s, Kaufmann's was a store for men and boys offering both ready-to-wear and custom-tailored clothing. Women could shop for their husbands or sons but not for themselves. Most women either made their own clothing or hired dressmakers because the ready-to-wear clothing that was available was often badly made and unfashionable.

In 1886, Kaufmann's began to sell and advertise women's shoes. By November, the store was advertising ladies' ready-made cloaks on sale and noted that they would also custom-tailor cloaks. These forays into women's clothing must have been successful. At the end of the year, when the store opened its "Grand Depot," it included a women's cloak department and installed red velvet carpeting to welcome women on "Ladies' Day." The brothers also hired their first woman to staff a lingerie department.

By December 1887, the store was carrying jackets and wraps, as well as cloaks. In an advertisement that ran in March 1889, the store described its manufacturers in Europe and seems to have been importing ready-to-wear clothing from France. An article in a Pittsburgh paper on September 22, 1889, described the fabrics that were available for custom-made women's clothing and how Jacob Kaufmann had purchased the fabrics in London, Paris, Berlin and Vienna.

By July 1890, the store had opened a corset department and in June was selling "waists" and separate skirts, which were wildly popular. Women

Kaufmann's began as a store selling clothing for men and boys. This catalogue from the late nineteenth century illustrates boys' suits that were available. Suits with kilts instead of trousers were popular in the late nineteenth century, at least with the parents who were doing the shopping.

had also embraced the practical "blazer suit"—a long skirt and jacket—and Kaufmann's had expanded its cloak department to include suits. It was clear that women would buy well-made clothing if it was affordable and stylish. As a February 22, 1890 Kaufmann's advertisement for jersey dresses commented, "At these prices it hardly pays to do your own dressmaking."

Women's clothing was just the beginning. In 1888, Kaufmann's added a "Photograph Gallery" that provided "no tintypes, mind you, but real, artistically mounted Photographs." In 1890, it added a grocery department and was advertising china and glass for sale for the Thanksgiving table. By the May 1897 anniversary, sales advertisements from Kaufmann's were selling a full range of clothing and household goods using the tagline "The Big Store."

From the time they first moved downtown, the Kaufmann brothers bought and leased surrounding properties with an eye toward expansion. As they increased their range of stock, they needed more selling space. They also added amenities to appeal to shoppers and to keep them in the store.

In 1881, the first elevator was installed in the store and promoted in advertisements. It could carry five people and two thousand pounds of

Left: Jackets and cloaks were among Kaufmann's first ready-made clothing sold for women. By December 1887, women's clothing was appearing in store advertisements.

Right: This clothing catalogue illustrates women's shirtwaists with extreme sleeves and skirts to wear with them. Skirts and "shirtwaists" were popular women's "ready-to-wear," and Kaufmann's sold them in a variety of styles and fabrics.

freight. Then, in 1882, the brothers bought the adjoining building and doubled the store's size. They erected a grand staircase that cost $300,000, and they advertised, "For the benefit of after dark purchasers, we have placed 9 electric burners, equal to 18,000 candle lights, making the interior of our store as bright as day."

In 1885, the store expanded again. Calling itself the "Grand Depot," it now boasted a tower topped by the Goddess of Liberty, whose flaming torch was fed by natural gas; 120 feet by 120 feet of street frontage; electric lights in front; and a huge, four-faced clock on a tall post. A sign on the clock encouraged shoppers to "Meet Me Under the Clock."

But the enlarged store was still not big enough. The Kaufmann brothers bought the "Old Home" church property in 1892 and leased nearby space to expand again. The expanded store debuted to the public in October 1898 with a grand opening themed "Triumphant America at Peace with All the World." A Pittsburgh newspaper article describing the new store claimed that it was now one of the largest in the country, almost as large as the new Wanamaker's in Philadelphia. Only three other stores in the country were larger, one each in Boston, New York and Chicago.

Kaufmann's downtown location became a busy shopping area. In this early image, shoppers can be seen crowding the sidewalks.

Kaufmann's now included "everything that the human family needs"—clothing, housewares, china, flowers, candy, books, millinery, jewelry and furniture. There were reception rooms, writing rooms and a lounge with couches for weary shoppers. In the basement, visitors could marvel at the new electric plant with its three Westinghouse dynamos, each one capable of powering four thousand lights. There was a pneumatic tube system to move money throughout the store. Kaufmann's now employed two thousand and added five hundred more for the holidays.

Shoppers and employees didn't even need to leave the store to eat. By 1889, Kaufmann's had a soda fountain at the foot of the stairs that served cherry cokes and sarsaparilla. With each soda, the buyer received a miniature charm to wear on a ribbon or to collect on a charm bracelet. For those who craved more than a soda, the store opened its New Vienna Café in March 1893. A *Pittsburgh Daily Post* reporter who attended the opening noted that it was one of the larger dining spaces in the city. Furnished in oak, it could seat 250. Dinners, served from 11:00 a.m. to 2:00 p.m., cost fifty cents; the restaurant would supply dinners at other times if ordered "by card." The opening meal for the press included predicable Victorian delicacies: oysters, terrapin and quail.

The store's success reflected the growing economy of Pittsburgh, but it also reflected the brothers' genius at marketing. In addition to newspaper advertising, the brothers embraced display windows and promotional events to lure shoppers. In the early days, clothing store windows might include a few bolts of fabric and nothing more. When Kaufmann's installed its first plate glass windows in 1886, it promised the public 208 feet of frontage with a "gigantic and gorgeous display." Windows included revolving mannequins that were turned by salesmen who worked out of sight in shifts. They also included educational displays; in March 1899, several toothpick manufacturing machines were operating in the Fifth Avenue windows, and anyone entering the store would be given a free packet of toothpicks.

The windows were used in concert with other promotions. "Look at our Mammoth Corner Window," trumpeted an advertisement during the fall of

FOSTER'S HOOK GLOVES

~FOR SALE BY~

KAUFMANN BROTHERS,
PITTSBURGH, PA.

MY LADY'S GLOVE

Women in the nineteenth and early twentieth centuries had wardrobes of gloves to accessorize every outfit. This small advertising card promotes a brand-name glove available at Kaufmann's.

1882. "This elegant rosewood piano free!" Everyone who bought a dollar's worth or more would be given a ticket for a chance on the free piano. The drawing was held at 4:00 p.m. on New Year's Day 1883 in front of three hundred people, none of whom held the winning ticket.

On November 30, 1883, the Kaufmann brothers tried a new promotion. In "The Great Clothing Shower," five thousand new pieces of men's and boy's clothing—coats, suits, trousers, hats—would be thrown from the roof of the store. The event was heavily advertised, and eighteen thousand people had gathered in front of the store that evening. At 6:45 p.m., by the glow of two calcium lights, twelve clerks began throwing packages wrapped in brown paper from the second-floor store windows. The "excited multitude" below fought for the packages, and at 7:15 p.m., thirty-five policemen broke up what had become a near riot. Pittsburgh's mayor asked the Kaufmann brothers to postpone the rest of the event. In the future, they distributed free clothing through social service agencies.

In 1884, the Kaufmann brothers returned to more staid promotions: "To Every Purchaser, we shall present a numbered ticket, entitling him to a chance to win a beautiful brocaded silk plush set of parlor furniture worth $500, an elegant phaeton and valuable horse with costly harness and bridle, worth $850 and a magnificent piano worth $600. Public Drawing will take place January 1, 1884, and the lucky number will be announced in the papers."

Rather than a public drawing for big-ticket items, the store tried a new promotion later in the year. Every purchaser received a "Little Brown Jug" with a slip of paper inside identifying a prize from small souvenirs to the biggest prize, a pony and cart. The "Little Brown Jug" promotion was repeated in 1886.

Instead of large drawings once a year, the Kaufmann brothers began to give regular premiums with purchase of goods. In the spring of 1884, it was a pocket watch with the purchase of a suit, a practice they continued for years and advertised heavily. They also gave away free circus tickets with a purchase one summer; free tickets to any Brotherhood Championship Game, including the opening baseball game where the Chicagos faced off against the Pittsburghs; stilts; baseball uniforms; and photographic sittings.

Special events, often tied to community interests or concerns, were also designed to attract shoppers. For example, in an era when food adulteration was common, Kaufmann's held a "Pure Food Show" in its grocery department. Suppliers set up booths where they demonstrated their products and gave free samples. The 18th Regiment Band provided a "Grand Concert" to open the event, which ran for several weeks.

Kaufmann's also used other promotions. In hot weather, it gave away free drinks of ice water at strategic corners in the city. It sent a brass band and boys into neighborhoods to distribute flyers on Saturdays and rewarded the boys with dinner—large sandwiches, pie and a pail of beer for a dime. In 1898, Kaufmann's started a semiannual free distribution of merchandise. A person with watch in hand sat near Smithfield Street and rang a gong every five minutes. The first customer who handed money to the store's only cashier after the gong sounded would have the money returned and pay nothing for the merchandise.

Kaufmann's also promoted itself across the region. The store offered free delivery service with distinctive mirrored horseshoe-shaped wagons and placed the message "This Car for Kaufmann's" on horse-drawn streetcars throughout the Pittsburgh area. Using the slogan "Everything Under the Sun," it had gigantic yellow suns haloed in orange painted on barns along every western Pennsylvania railroad line.

By 1900, Kaufmann's was ready to enter the new century as a full-fledged department store.

Chapter 2

THE BIG STORE

*B*y the turn of the twentieth century, Kaufmann's "The Big Store" was well on its way to becoming a classic example of the newest form of retailing: the department store. During the first two decades of the new century, the brothers would consolidate and expand their business into the store that later generations would fondly remember. The expansion was driven by changes within the Kaufmann family and by new business practices.

The four founding brothers were still actively involved in the business, but they were bringing in the next generation of the family to help. Jacob had four sons who may have been involved in the store's real estate transactions. Isaac had two sons: Edgar Jonas, or E.J., who began working in the store in 1909, and the much younger Oliver. The other two brothers had daughters. Morris's daughters would marry men who later joined the store, including Samuel Mundheim and Ira Wolf. Henry had only one child, daughter Irene.

The brothers also welcomed at least seven Kaufmann and Baer cousins from Germany who joined the business. One of the cousins, Morris Baer, had become the general manager of the store by 1913. Then, on November 1, 1905, Jacob, fifty-six, died unexpectedly following surgery for appendicitis. He had been ill and had traveled to Philadelphia to see a specialist, who diagnosed the disease. The surgery, performed by four prominent surgeons, went well, and Jacob seemed to be recovering. His brothers returned to Pittsburgh only to be informed by telegram that Jacob was dead. The store was closed immediately.

9522 Kaufmann's - "The Big Store" - Pittsburg.

Kaufmann's also used the slogan "The Big Store" to emphasize its large selection of merchandise.

Jacob's death was followed less than two years later by the death of Henry's only daughter, Irene. When her father was told, again by telegram, to come immediately to the family's summer house in New Jersey, he thought that Irene, an avid "motorist," had been hurt in a car crash. By the time he arrived, she was already dead. As the newspapers reported the next day, July 24, 1907, she had mistakenly drunk carbolic acid thinking it was headache medicine. The stories claimed that she was in high spirits, that she planned to have lunch with friends and that her maid was with her and saw everything, but stories persisted that it was a suicide.

A black-edged advertisement announced that the store would be closed for two days. Henry and his wife, Emma, were devastated. To assuage their grief, they established a memorial, the Irene Kaufmann Settlement House, in Pittsburgh's Hill District.

Almost two years later, on June 23, 1909, there was a happier event that would have major implications for the store. E.J. Kaufmann married his cousin Lillian, Morris's daughter, in New York. By the time of his marriage, E.J. had a solid career in the store. He was well educated with a degree from Yale and had worked in two European department stores, Hamburg's Karstadt and Galeries Lafayette in Paris. His surviving uncles respected his business acumen.

E.J. Kaufmann (the driver), son of Isaac Kaufmann, one of the founding brothers, joined the family business in 1909 as an assistant shipping clerk. He had worked at Marshall Field's in Chicago, the Galleries LaFayette in Paris and the Karstadt Department Stores in Hamburg before returning to Pittsburgh. After becoming president of Kaufmann's in 1924, his initiatives included the International Exposition of Arts and Industry and the "Peaks of Progress."

It may have been E.J. who suggested incorporating the store in January 1913. Newspapers reported that the move was made to safeguard the future of the store and allow employees to participate in its profits. Kaufmann's had its best year in 1912 and used its positive financial performance to sell its new stock. The incorporation also ensured E.J.'s future. Because of inheritance arrangements within the family, he and his wife, Lillian, controlled a substantial amount of stock. They may have purchased the stock of Jacob's sons and their Uncle Henry. In any case, Jacob's sons established a realty company, and Henry focused on his charitable activities, leaving E.J. to focus on the store.

The Kaufmann and Baer cousins were not part of the incorporation. Led by Morris Baer, they quit and founded their own department store, Kaufmann & Baer, taking many Kaufmann's employees with them. In 1913, they built a huge new $25 million store a few blocks away at Smithfield and Sixth. From descriptions in the press, it's clear that they modeled the new store on Kaufmann's.

By the time Lillian's father, Morris Kaufmann, died in 1917 and E.J.'s father, Isaac, died in 1921, Kaufmann's was in good hands.

E.J.'s growing influence on the store was apparent before 1920. Educated and cosmopolitan, he was interested in technology, art, architecture and fashion. He was willing to spend to improve the store. He valued exhibitions, public lectures and quality entertainment to entice people into the store while providing a public benefit. Under his leadership, Kaufmann's evolved from the popular-priced store to the fashion-forward retailer of high-quality merchandise.

In the early twentieth century, Kaufmann's continued to expand its physical infrastructure. In September 1900, the store bought the old Oregon Brewery property at the corner of Forbes and Stevenson and built its first warehouse. The nine-story building planned for the site was designed as

Department stores offered delivery services from the earliest days. Horses and wagons were kept in Kaufmann's first warehouse, which contained an elevator large enough to hold a loaded delivery wagon.

a combination stable/wagon house and storage facility. It had 250 horse stalls in the basement and included "all the latest sanitary and time-saving appliances for modern stables." Delivery wagons were kept on the first floor. The building featured huge elevators that could accommodate a fully loaded wagon; wagons could be loaded inside the building instead of on the street. Furniture was stored on the upper floors.

Despite the "time-saving appliances for modern stables," maintaining a fleet of horses and wagons was expensive. By August 1906, Kaufmann's had taken delivery of its first two automobiles, with six more on order. In July 1911, it ordered twelve additional Packard trucks to complement those already in the fleet. As the *Pittsburgh Post Gazette* commented about the trucks, "The excellent service rendered has demonstrated that automobile delivery is more efficient and cheaper than horse delivery." By 1912, the store had twenty Packards. Although Kaufmann's would continue to advertise for stable help through the end of the decade, trucks were quickly replacing horses, especially for quick deliveries to outlying regions. In June 1913, the store replaced fourteen Packards with twenty-three new White trucks.

In 1900, Kaufmann's constructed a state-of-the-art stable and warehouse with room to house 250 horses in basement stalls. Delivery wagons were kept on the first floor, and upper floors of the nine-story building were used to store furniture. Delivery wagons could be loaded inside the building instead of on the street.

In 1921, the Delivery Department employed seventy-one people, including drivers, who were called "chauffeurs." Boys were hired to assist the drivers. Kaufmann's touted the safe driving records of its chauffeurs in the press.

Kaufmann's was one of the first stores in Pittsburgh to replace its horses and wagons with delivery trucks to save money, especially on long-distance deliveries. This truck was one of the first in its new delivery fleet.

Kaufmann's had also outgrown its warehouse. By 1902, the store was selling furniture, and the booming furniture business required more storage. In a March 1913 advertisement, Kaufmann's announced that it was building a new warehouse on Water Street on the city's North Side. The warehouse would provide three and a half acres of floor space directly on a rail line so that cars could unload on a siding next to the building. The old warehouse would now be used solely as a garage.

In 1912, the downtown store expanded again from four connected buildings ranging from five to twelve floors to a massive new store that filled the entire block. E.J. selected architect Benno Janssen to design a new addition that would replace the building on Fifth Avenue that would be demolished.

During demolition of the eight-story building, engineers attached ropes to the four wheels of a wagon and hoisted it to the roof using a derrick on an adjoining building. When it was full, it was lowered to the street. The store

The store was expanded in 1912 and the interior and exterior spaces remodeled. Here banners announce a rebuilding sale; sales were held regularly during the expansion. The original Kaufmann's clock can be seen on the corner.

remained open during demolition and construction, with stock shifted as needed. As each department was moved to its new location, advertisements encouraged shoppers to visit the new spaces.

In December 1913, a newspaper commented, "If it is something pertaining to department stores…Kaufmann's is sure to have it first." In this case, it was the first escalator in the city. The reporter described his experience: a smiling young man in a uniform announced, "Going up?—step on the escalator, please." Then he gently guided people to the "Moving Stairway," placed their hands on the rail and, as the reporter related, "just about the time our timidness wears off and we are enjoying the novelty of the thing, we are at the top." For those who couldn't handle the novelty, the store installed twenty-four elevators.

The new store had room not only for more merchandise but also for more services. There were credit accounts; in a January 1, 1914 advertisement for the store's fur sale, shoppers were reminded that they could open an account and buy a fur on time. Credit was also encouraged for buyers of sewing machines and refrigerators. As early as 1905, there was a hair salon that offered shampoos, hairdressing and manicures, as well as Marcel and French waves. For a brief period, Carnegie Library had a "call station" in the store where shoppers could pick up and return books. Shoppers so overwhelmed the service that it was closed after two years.

One of the most interesting services was what the store called its "Foreign Department." Pittsburgh at the time had one of the most diverse communities in the country, with scores of immigrants. The Foreign Department was designed to help these immigrant shoppers as well as foreign visitors and provide support for store buyers overseas. Multilingual store employees could translate for shoppers who spoke German, French, Italian, Russian, Polish, Slovak, Serbian, Lithuanian, Hungarian or Ruthenian. In the past, store owners had often taken advantage of immigrants, but "[t]oday that same foreign born…buys…at 'The Big Store' and…receives equal service and courtesy as an American millionaire."

To attract people to the store, Kaufmann's continued to advertise heavily in the local newspapers, running its first full-page newspaper ad in 1902. But it also began to focus on its large windows and to stage exhibitions and events to entertain and educate the public. Other stores may have been content to display merchandise in their windows, but not Kaufmann's. In September 1907, people flocked to the store windows to see two live bear cubs, Teddy and Mollie. The cubs, which had first lived in shipping crate dens on the store roof, had been brought to the city by a pastor who summered in Canada.

After spending several weeks in the Fifth Avenue windows, the cubs were donated to the Pittsburgh Zoo.

In 1912, thousands of people crowded the windows to watch a mechanical "Mystic Rollers" device drop ammonia on two brass beds, one finished with "Damard Lacquer" and one without. The machine also flashed cards with an explanation of the display—the lacquered bed was guaranteed to resist ammonia, used to remove fly specks, for five years. The machine also used cards to show the transformation of an early sleeper sofa into a bed. Apparently, the crowds weren't as interested in the message as they were in how the machine operated. Later that year, glass was actually removed to install a Mercedes Blitzen II race car in the windows. The fastest car in the world, it was displayed with the $10,000 Speed King crown and Remy Brassard trophy.

Displays and exhibitions were staged inside the store as well, not only to attract the public but also to educate them. They often included a technology component. For example, in April 1900, the store showed moving pictures of the pope in his daily life and in the Vatican to huge crowds; people paid a nickel each to attend. The money raised was donated to local orphanages. Several years later, visitors were invited to "panoramic representations" of the history of the Johnstown Flood.

After the bears in the window, animals continued to be a big draw. In April 1905, trick horse Bonner performed 150 different feats in the store's amusement hall. He was followed in the fall by three Shetland ponies that danced a quadrille, waltzed on their hind legs and played on a seesaw. In June 1909, "'possoms" were on display, described as "Taft's favorite food in South." The opossums, a mother and eleven babies, lived in a large cage in the toy department after arriving on a train from North Carolina.

Kaufmann's also continued its interest in new technology. In October 1909, a full-size reproduction of the Curtiss biplane was placed on display along with six-foot models of six other airships, including the Chanute glider, Zeppelin, Bleriot monoplane and Wright biplane. Hourly lectures explained the technologies. The display was so popular that the store held the exhibit over for an additional week. The next year, thousands flocked to see an exact replica of the Wright airplane suspended from the ceiling with the motor running and the propellers turning.

Events were also held in individual departments, including recitals in the piano department and photo developing by Kodak experts in the camera department. The sports equipment department was a popular venue for these events featuring "fancy bag punching and scientific boxing" by a local boxer, demonstration of a home gymnasium machine that would deliver "rich, red blood, tough sinews, and pink condition" and a series of golf tournaments at the store's indoor practice course.

But the shipping department was responsible for one of the store's most brilliant promotional events. When Harry Houdini was appearing in Pittsburgh, the packers challenged him to get out of a shipping box that they had nailed shut and tied with ropes. The catch: he couldn't demolish the box. Houdini accepted, and an October 5, 1906, article in a Pittsburgh paper described the result. The packers nailed Houdini in the box while five thousand people watched. The theater was so crowded that hundreds were turned away. The floor had been inspected and a carpet placed

Kaufmann's used catalogues to encourage mail-order shopping by those who lived too far away to shop in Downtown Pittsburgh. This stylebook from 1917 shows that women's clothing was beginning to change from the heavy suits and long skirts worn in the late nineteenth and early twentieth centuries.

down so that Houdini could not escape through a trapdoor. In exactly fourteen minutes, he stepped from behind a curtain that surrounded the box, minus his coat. When the box, still tightly nailed, was broken open, Houdini's coat was inside.

Events were also key in positioning the store as a fashion destination. In 1921, E.J. Kaufmann recalled working as a floor man early in his career: "In those days we were the popular-priced store. It was Kaufmann's that had the cheapest merchandise. It was Kaufmann's that carried inferior and cheap brands." As he became more influential, that changed. It may have started with the millinery, a large and profitable department early in the century. Women had wardrobes of hats, and the most fashionable came from Europe. Hat fashions changed with the seasons, and women yearned for the newest creations. They were also willing to spend for hats: one Kaufmann's advertisement listed imported hats at $50 to $125.

Hats were an obsession of fashionable women. By 1911, Kaufmann's was holding exhibitions of the latest millinery from Europe that may have developed into the store's later fashion "promenades," or fashion shows. Local press covered the events in detail. Invitations like this were sent to store patrons to encourage them to attend.

By March 1911, the store was using a model to show hats from Vienna, London, Paris and New York to Pittsburgh women, who crowded the millinery exhibition. The press reported the event, providing details on styles and colors for those who could not attend. "King's blue"—a reference to the upcoming coronation of King George—was a popular choice. The event was so popular that Kaufmann's repeated it in the fall. This time, the press sent an artist to sketch the hats that had just arrived from Paris and to interview the buyer a week before the event. One of the innovations of the season, she noted, was the small hat popular with women who "motor" because the wind wouldn't dislodge it. Other hats illustrating the article were so large that it would be hard to imagine walking in them on the windy streets of Pittsburgh, let alone "motoring."

Gowns were also exhibited in the store and discussed in the press as early as 1909. In 1911, a writer covered an event that she dubbed the "trouser skirt problem." A model had visited Kaufmann's to introduce the new trouser skirt, an innovation that she described as practical—"just fancy the luxury of having pockets." She went on to note, "And as for comfort...ladies, unless you've 'dressed up' in your brother's or husband's clothes, you don't know what freedom of motion means." The illustration of the model shows what we would call a split skirt, worn with a period suit jacket and mandatory hat. While clever and comfortable, the trouser suit wouldn't become popular until decades in the future.

It wasn't long before single models gave way to full-fledged in-store fashion shows. Kaufmann's seems to have conducted its first in March 1913. A local fashion writer described the "fashion promenade" at the store as an "entirely new idea," with a lighted and decorated stage, thirty professional models from New York and an orchestra. Using changing scenes instead of runway walks, the models wore the latest Paris styles: afternoon dresses, evening gowns, wedding clothes and "black and now fashionable white mourning." There were sports clothes for riding, tennis and golf and dresses for children and schoolgirls. All of the gowns were shown with hats made in the store.

The show, now called a "Fashion Play," was repeated in the fall and soon became a regular event. In March 1914, the setting was an Italian garden with ferns and palms, and the models presented fashions for the boulevard,

Modest and practical, ladies' suits were popular in the late nineteenth and early twentieth centuries when almost all women owned at least one. Kaufmann's Ladies' Suit Department offered custom tailoring to women in 1910.

the opera and an evening of cards. In October 1914, the "Fashion Play" presented "scenes from the Fashionable woman's daily life," including a "Dansant," "The Horse Show" and "The Country Club."

It was not only a "Style Promenade" but also a message about how the store thought that its shoppers spent their days. At the time, the upper classes attended horse shows and belonged to the country club, not the middle classes. But those middle-class shoppers were being schooled to become aspirational consumers.

Kaufmann's also used educational events to position itself as a fashion store, although the content of some might seem strange to us today. In 1909, a local female reporter headlined her piece on a Kaufmann event, "Fat Women Can Be Shapely, If They Wear Nemo Corsets." She went on to describe in detail how Madame, a nationally recognized corsetiere, taught women how to properly fit their corsets, including one, a "self-reducing model," that was so comfortable "[y]ou could scrub floors in this corset without any trouble."

Several years later, the corset event was followed by a series of beauty lectures sponsored by the cosmetic department, then called toilet goods, at Kaufmann's. Although the event was free, those interested had to pick up tickets at the store, and Madame-endorsed products sold there. While many of the lectures apparently focused on staying youthful, one was called "How to Marry Scientifically."

Dining in the store also became an event. In 1914, the New Vienna Café evolved into a full-scale restaurant, with mahogany furniture, crystal chandeliers, thick carpeting, linen tablecloths, heavy silver and city views. Prices were reasonable, reported the press. Kaufmann's ads regularly featured restaurant specials: roast beef in the "Opportunity Day Luncheon," lobster in the "Velvet Beach Luncheon" and fried chicken in the "Louisiana Luncheon." An advertisement in July 1914 for the "'Aristocrat' Luncheon" of lamb and vegetable casserole touted the restaurant as the "Coolest Spot in Pittsburgh" and bragged that "not a fly" was in sight.

With its embrace of technology, fashion and gracious living and its growing emphasis on youth, Kaufmann's was poised to enter a period that later historians would see as the high point of the department store: the 1920s.

Chapter 3

A Modern Department Store

*I*n 1921, Kaufmann's celebrated its fiftieth anniversary with golden décor. The largest department store in Pittsburgh, it had come a long way from its humble roots on the South Side. It now covered an entire city block with 750,000 square feet on twelve retail floors.

On the first floor, decorators painted the pillars gold, placed gold foliage arrangements on the counters and used gold in the windows, which displayed items used when the store was founded in 1871. Merchandise was tagged with anniversary prices on gold tickets. The centerpiece was an eight-foot loving cup made of white, pink and red roses and filled with American Beauty roses, a gift to management from the employees. Each employee wore a golden rose.

When the doors opened at 8:30 a.m., the public was waiting eagerly outside for the sale. Later, a formal dinner was served for friends of the store in the restaurant on the Eleventh Floor, with Metropolitan Opera star Anna Cass providing entertainment. Concerts for the public featured singers, a harpist and pianists, including Percy Grainger.

Kaufmann's had also changed in ways that shoppers from 1890 would have noticed. Pneumatic cash-moving tubes, the first installed in the city, had replaced cash boys and cash girls. While there were still horses and wagons in the delivery service, the store now had a large fleet of trucks. Fashionable women still demanded hats, and the store's French millinery workroom employed thirty-two people. The store still had a grocery department, but it would close in a year, faced with competition from chain groceries.

Women were responsible for some of the biggest changes. They shed their heavy corsets, layers of petticoats, long skirts, dark stockings and laced boots. They cut their hair. They started to wear makeup. They began doing more of their own housework.

Prosperity allowed shoppers to buy, but there was competition for those shopping dollars. People who had electrified their houses wanted electrical appliances and now had to pay utility bills. Cars, telephones, an hour at the beauty shop—the lure of modernity meant less to spend on other things. The newly instituted income tax also reduced disposable income.

Auto horn ad from 1920s. Kaufmann's had an auto accessory department by 1907. The store promised customers that it would not take advantage of automobile owners because they were rich enough to afford a car.

Department stores modernized and added services to attract shoppers—tearooms and lounges, lending libraries, beauty shops and interior decorating services. In 1920, Kaufmann's hired a woman to advise customers on interior decorating. At the Adoria Beauty Salon, attendants in canary yellow dresses with crisp organdy collars and cuffs provided the latest waves for bobbed hair. Kaufmann's offered a parking service for cars with uniformed attendants. Using a direct line to the garage, shoppers could call for their cars. Their packages would be waiting for them at the garage.

Kaufmann's clerks did not hand packages directly to customers unless they had permission from the floor walker. Instead, packages were sent to a parcel room, where shoppers could retrieve them. And if shoppers didn't want to be burdened, there was home delivery—so fast that shoppers who bought merchandise in the morning would find the package waiting when they arrived home later in the day. To perform this feat, Kaufmann's maintained a fleet of one hundred trucks at its Forbes Street Service Station.

Stores also began offering more credit and installment plans to encourage spending, especially on big-ticket items. Kaufmann's advertised "Kelvinator" electric washing machines, stoves and refrigerators that could be purchased on installment plans. Its new consumers believed that buying fashionable things could bring status, success and happiness and a life that was modern, convenient and beautiful.

Kaufmann's literally searched the globe to fulfill shoppers' desires for merchandise. The Kaufmann brothers had regularly gone to Europe on buying trips. Now the store had foreign buying offices in twenty-seven cities in Europe and the East. As the Kaufmann's internal magazine, the *Storagram* noted, in this way "Kaufmann buyers of style merchandise secure for Pittsburgh women authentic styles and full range of the mode."

Another *Storagram* writer compared contemporary shopping with the past in 1927: "Could milady alight from her motor and spend an entire day amid imported hats and gowns—or could she purchase charming frocks for her small daughter, linens for her table, furniture for every room of her house, or objects of art for the choicest of gift occasions? Could the home maker come to Kaufmann's in 1879 and see in the store a veritable house charming

Sewing machines were expensive and were one of the first items that could be bought on credit. This display from the International Exposition of Arts and Industries shows the latest in sewing machine technology in 1926.

SPORTS WEAR FOR 1927
As Presented by Kaufmann's Sports Shop

IT is sports wear today, we venture to declare, which reflects more than anything in the realm of clothes, what advancement women have made since 1871, toward freedom, common sense and the full joy of living. Sports wear is outstandingly the contribution of the last few years to the history of costuming. We feel proud that our generation has created this particular type of apparel—a style that has the utmost ease and grace—a style that is colorful, gay, joyous—a style that bespeaks the vigorous, glad-to-be-alive American girl.

The sketch above presents correct apparel for the full cycle of a day at the country club, where smart sports wear is to be seen at its best. Kaufmann's Sports Shop offers distinctive imports from England and France, as well as those delightful creations that come from American designers whose specialty is youth-giving sports apparel.

By 1927, women's clothing had changed radically. After World War I, women shed their long skirts, dark stockings and boots. They bobbed their hair. Stores embraced fashion to sell to "modern" women, holding fashion shows and hiring women for their fashion expertise. This advertisement positions Kaufmann's as a fashion-forward store.

with all its rooms furnished and arranged to allow the furniture exactly as it would look in her own home?"

E.J., who became president of Kaufmann's in 1924, understood the department store business, how it was changing and how to manage accordingly. It helped that he and his wife personified modern tastemakers. E.J. and Liliane (she had changed her name from Lillian) lived in an eighteen-room Norman mansion in Fox Chapel, an upscale Pittsburgh suburb, where they had a large greenhouse for orchids. They were active in steeplechasing and collected art. Liliane loved fashion. They traveled to Europe regularly.

E.J. had been actively working at Kaufmann's during the first two decades of the new century; changes in the store may have reflected his influence. Now those changes continued. The store hired a stylist to advise buyers of changing fashions in children's clothing. It added a Travel Bureau, a barbershop, a new camera department and a picture department that sold framed art. E.J. hired a Hungarian architect and stage designer, Lazlo Garger, to design interior displays and show windows. The move was expensive, but Kaufmann's had some of the best window displays in the country.

Kaufmann's was nationally known for its artistic store windows, some of the best in the country at the time. This Art Deco window reflects the interior design of the store's first floor.

Fashion shows, first called Fashion Plays, were big events in the 1920s. Kaufmann's continued to stage fashion shows as late as the 1990s, both to showcase the store's merchandise and to support charity benefits.

In September 1925, the Adoria Beauty Salon opened with fifteen manicurists and thirty other employees. The salon provided staff to the "Bobber Shop" on the third floor, where women could shed their long hair for recently introduced "finger waves." There was an "Ann Adams" Service for telephone and mail-order customers, as well as personal shopping. It's not clear if former president Taft phoned Ann Adams, but when he was in Pittsburgh and needed a pair of white flannel trousers in a hurry, Kaufmann's had his large size in stock.

E.J. continued his interest in technology and his willingness to bring it to the store. In 1924, he added "the greatest escalator system in the world," with moving stairways from the first to the tenth floors. The escalators could carry forty thousand people per day; female shoppers appreciated their safety, speed and lack of congestion.

In March 1928, E.J. made the first long-distance call from Pittsburgh to Paris, just hours after ATT put the transatlantic circuit into service. With

The store auditorium, set up for a book signing in the 1920s. Book signings and Book and Author Dinners were popular events at Kaufmann's. Many other events were also staged in the auditorium.

the press watching, he spoke to the store's representatives in the fashion city. With Paris now a phone call away, the store could keep abreast of fast-changing fashion.

Emphasis on fashion continued as well with regular fashion shows and events. During an October 1925 event in the misses' coat department, four artists from local colleges painted popular cartoon characters on the backs of rain slickers; "Krazy Kat" was the most popular. In 1926, the store also started a series of fashion articles by Paris designers like Jean Patou sent by "special cable."

E.J. had always favored educational exhibits over hard selling. His interest in modernism and art put Kaufmann's on the national map in the 1920s. In 1925, the Art Deco exhibition in Paris had launched a new design trend and inspired international attention to modernism. E.J. knew that Paris department stores had participated in the exhibition. He also knew that the U.S. government feared that the lack of artistic design in American products would affect its ability to compete in world markets.

In 1926, Kaufmann's sponsored the International Exposition of Arts and Industries to showcase industrial processes and good design. As curator of the Brooklyn Museum, Stewart Culin, pointed out during a speech at the store, "The department store stands for the greatest influences for taste and culture that exist today in America." For every person who went to a museum to see new things, ten thousand went to department stores.

As E.J. commented, "No modern organization is in a better position to observe this artistic evolution than a large department store. Close contact with the varied demands of human beings has indicated to us the public's increasing appreciation of color and form, the dollar is no longer the sole issue."

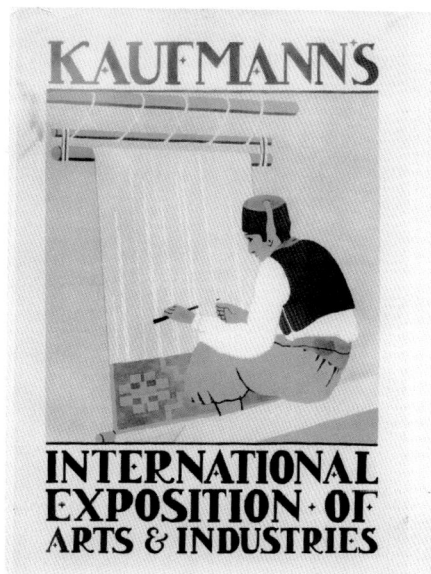

The International Exposition of Arts and Industries, staged at Kaufmann's in 1926, drew national attention to the store. It included educational displays and technology demonstrations.

The exhibition was a mixed display of industrial processes and artful objects. Visitors could see how stockings, gloves, enamelware and linoleum were made. They could see one of Abraham Lincoln's high silk hats and the first dollar watch made in America, as well as original Paris gowns and Lalique glass made for the exhibit. There was a "Palace of Silks" from around the world, Filipino women making fine embroidery in a re-created native hut and a weaver making sunroom furniture.

The event was repeated in following years, with contests for schoolchildren, adults and women's clubs; Art in Industry lectures; banquets; and concerts. Exhibits were also staged throughout the selling departments. "The First Photoradiogram Machine Ever Exhibited in Any Retail Store Now in Operation on Our 4th Floor," stated one newspaper advertisement. The machine, from RCA and Westinghouse, was similar to a modern fax machine and could send a picture over the radio waves. In this way, the store could receive fashion photos and drawings from London, Paris and New York. Other exhibits in the store included Beethoven's piano and the guns Byrd took to the North Pole.

Industrial displays were a key feature of the exposition. E.J. Kaufmann, president of Kaufmann's, preferred educational marketing to hard selling.

Regular Kaufmann's suppliers were invited to display merchandise during the International Exposition of Arts and Industries. Mirro, once the world's largest manufacturer of aluminum cooking utensils, staged this exhibition of its products. At the time, aluminum cooking utensils were relatively new and were replacing more traditional materials like cast iron.

E.J.'s interest in art as applied to commerce also drove a major redesign of the store's first floor in 1930. The project cost more than $2.5 million and was an Art Deco masterpiece.

Architect Benno Janssen and his partner William Cocken designed the first floor like the spokes of a wheel, with aisles radiating from elevators in the center. The design, which may have been suggested by E.J., was scientifically planned to encourage efficient shopping, and all of the service features were hidden. Shoppers saw only black Carrara glass columns, bronze metalwork, the latest terrazzo floors and fixtures of pale avodire wood from Africa. They didn't notice strategically located wrapping desks and termini for four charge tubes. They may not have paid attention to ninety-six new black National Cash Registers carefully worked into the floor plan so that clerks would have to take the fewest possible steps to them to ring up sales.

The metrics of the design were amazing. To encase the pillars, workers had to grind and polish forty tons of PPG glass—8,230 separate pieces. To engrave the floral decorations on the metal arcade grills, a team of specially trained artisans came from France. All of the metallic elements—grills, elevator doors, railings, drinking fountains, flower sconces and clocks—were designed and fabricated locally.

The stunning design masked equally impressive engineering. A new ceiling was constructed just to contain miles of pipes for a new firefighting system. Quartz bulbs would melt and engage the sprinklers when the temperature reached 135 degrees Fahrenheit. Linear lighting used ten thousand Westinghouse Mazda lamps, replacing old-fashioned pendant lights. Ducts under the floors carried three hundred miles of wiring for lights, heat and telephones. As a reporter noted, "Television, when it becomes commercially feasible, is also provided for by this new system of wiring." There was an electrical outlet every two feet, and power was provided by the largest transformer vaults in any retail store. Huge beams of structural steel had been used to reinforce the floors.

To deal with Pittsburgh's smog and humidity, Kaufmann's installed a state-of-the-art ventilating and "refrigerating system" that could condition 10.8 million cubic feet of air every hour. It provided cooling equivalent to 800,000 pounds of melting ice each day.

And there were more escalators, the world's largest installation of the technology to date from Otis Elevator. Escalators had proved their worth during the store's heavy holiday rushes, so the new design called for sixty-six separate escalators ranged in three double banks running up and down from the basement store to the thirteenth floor. These "winged

The photoradio machine used radio to transmit photographs. An early fax technology, Kaufmann's used it to receive the latest fashion designs from its Paris offices.

stairways" cost more than $1 million and could handle 1,684,000 shoppers daily.

If the design were not enough to impress, E.J. commissioned well-known muralist Boardman Robinson to paint a series of ten murals averaging fifteen by eight feet. The murals, entitled "Art in Industry," depicted the history of commerce through the ages. They were placed just below the ceiling.

2nd Floor - Diamond St. Side - toward Smithfield St.

MELLON-STUART COMPANY
Contracting Engineers
Pittsburgh, Pa.
KAUFMANN ALTERATION JOB
No. 24   Date 8-24-29
Photographed by
JOHNSTON & JOHNSTON, Inc

Motor platform
Escalator trusses   New Stairs
Escalator step

2nd Floor - 5th Ave. side - toward 5th Ave. and Smithfield St.

MELLON-STUART COMPANY
Contracting Engineers
Pittsburgh, Pa.
KAUFMANN ALTERATION JOB
No. 1752-0   Date 5-21-29
Photo by Trinity Court Studio
E. W. JOHNSTON

Above: The Boardman Robinson murals charted the history of commerce. They were first installed when the first floor of Kaufmann's was redesigned in 1930. Postcards of all the murals were sold in the store, and individual cards were distributed in convention packets to encourage Pittsburgh visitors to shop at Kaufmann's.

Opposite, top: Kaufmann's was one of the first department stores in the country to install escalators. The magical "moving stairways" were heavily advertised and supposedly appealed to women because they were safe and hygienic.

Opposite, bottom: Engineers installed this state-of-the-art escalator technology in 1929. Decades later, shoppers could still ride the early wooden escalators on Kaufmann's upper floors.

The newly designed floor was officially opened in May 1930. In an article, a reporter gushed, "Yes, beautiful it is. And convenient too. Convenient in a daring, revolutionary way…On guard! No dear reader, this isn't an exercise in wartime—it's the rallying call of the innumerable array of gadgets, widgets or what-you-will, seated high above your unsuspecting heads—in the ceiling of the new First and Arcade Floors. The sprinkler heads! The little quartz bulbs! The wet army! In short—the Grinnell fire-fighting apparatus—always on guard, while you shop in complete security in the Store of Stores—Kaufmann's."

At the same time, the Pittsburgh papers carried unsettling news about the stock markets and the economic future of the country. On December 29, 1929, one of them asked E.J. about his thoughts on the future. "The outlook for next year is favorable," he commented, "and should be as good as 1929…The country and its industries are economically sound. The only problem we have to face is to keep our people employed."

Chapter 4

SURVIVING THE DEPRESSION

*I*n early 1930, Kaufmann's unveiled the Boardman Robinson murals in a series of evening festivities—one night for store executives and special guests, including the governor of Pennsylvania; one for store employees and their families; and another for the workers who had created the modern first floor and their families. The murals were unveiled one at a time by the wives of the artist, store executives and politicians. The national press was invited, and 274 news outlets sent their art editors to the event.

On Thursday morning at 10:00 a.m., the murals were unveiled for the public. The store had booklets printed with the history of the murals and descriptions of the different panels and distributed 50,000 of them in the first month. It printed postcards as well. Shoppers could buy the set for a quarter. To attract out-of-town visitors, a postcard was included in the delegate packages for all conventions in the city; the store distributed 100,000 postcards to potential visitors in a single year. The cards were used in art schools, and the murals were used in the store's institutional advertising.

The murals seemed to symbolize the store's optimism for the new decade. There was troubling economic news in the press, but Kaufmann's had been very profitable in 1929 and didn't see any immediate threat to its business. On February 22, 1930, E.J. Kaufmann sent 150 store buyers to a daylong retreat at Carnegie Museum for lectures and inspiration; art would help them select merchandise. No one suspected that in the upcoming years that price would be more important than design.

The Depression of the 1930s was a challenge to department stores. They had catered to women with lavish services, higher-priced quality goods and attractive downtown stores. Now the purchasing power of the middle class declined dramatically, and people became price-conscious. Many were unemployed. Stores that survived—and many did not—had to react creatively. Kaufmann's did.

By 1932, the store was among the first to comply with the National Recovery Act requirement for a forty-hour week. In March 1932, Kaufmann's reported a sales volume record, but purchasing power in the community had decreased and so had the total dollar value of sales for the previous year. The store admitted trimming expenses. But considering that national department store sales dropped 41 percent between 1929 and 1933, it was in relatively good shape.

Its redesigned first floor attracted shoppers and reduced costs. The new fluorescent lights were not only cooler but also cheaper to run. The new design featured popular merchandise—cosmetics, accessories, jewelry,

Kaufmann's got national attention for its Art Deco first floor, installed in 1930. The aisles were set up like spokes of a wheel to encourage efficient shopping, an idea that was attributed to E.J. Kaufmann.

candy and handkerchiefs—that was often bought as a small luxury. Half of the transactions that happened on the first floor of a store could account for one-third of its profits.

By 1933, it was clear that what may have looked like a temporary economic decline was more serious. Unemployment was a critical issue, and E.J. Kaufmann developed the "Pittsburgh Plan" to provide work relief instead of an outright dole payment to the unemployed. The plan was adopted in Allegheny County and got the attention of leaders in Harrisburg and Washington, D.C. He was also concerned about his employees. In a 1935 *Storagram*, he wrote, "The Management has endeavored to keep the morale, the good fellowship, and the contentment of our fellow-workers through these rather difficult years of adjustment."

Management also seemed to understand that store customers were no longer living the consumer lifestyles that they had been before the crash. There were no more fashion shows assuming that "milady" had maids at home so that she could spend the day at the country club or horse show. Advertisements were more like those of Kaufmann's past, offering practical, affordable merchandise at sale prices. The store bought stock from failing businesses and passed along the savings to the public at special sales.

While it focused on price, Kaufmann's understood that its middle-class customers wanted to maintain the illusion that they had not fallen into poverty. The store continued to advertise automobile accessories and golf equipment. An advertisement encouraged drivers to install the latest in car radio technology. An Epicure Shop that replaced its grocery sold gourmet foods. While it rarely advertised furs for sale, the store provided an off-season service to re-line, redesign and repair furs for customers to keep store furriers employed.

Kaufmann's had always stressed value. Now it underscored those claims with scientific evidence. The store had established a Kaufmann Fellowship at Mellon Institute to underwrite scientific support of merchandizing and sales promotion and to develop new products. The first product was an improved dry cleaning fluid.

By the early 1930s, a team of 116 specialists working under the leadership of Dr. Jules Labarthe had evaluated fifty-six different products. Their work allowed the store to choose the best materials for store-brand items and to test new products like laundry detergents. For example, the team evaluated fabrics to use in boys' shirts, washing samples forty-five times and then measuring shrinkage. It also tested linens, cosmetics, handkerchiefs, electric

For decades, Kaufmann's was a full-service store, selling hardware, paint, wallpaper and garden supplies, as well as clothing. Hardware departments were phased out when department stores could not compete with discount stores.

Electrical appliances became strong sellers in the 1920s, and demand continued throughout the Depression. Kaufmann's housewares department offered customers a huge selection of small household appliances.

refrigerators and paints. It tested clothing to determine that the fabric content was accurate; suits labeled 100 percent wool had to be wool.

Scientists also investigated customer complaints. If an item was returned to the store as damaged, it would be sent for testing. If the fault was in the product, the customer would be reimbursed. But scientists

During the Depression, Kaufmann's stressed the value of its merchandise, not just the price. The store established a fellowship at Mellon Institute, where teams of scientists developed new products and evaluated existing ones.

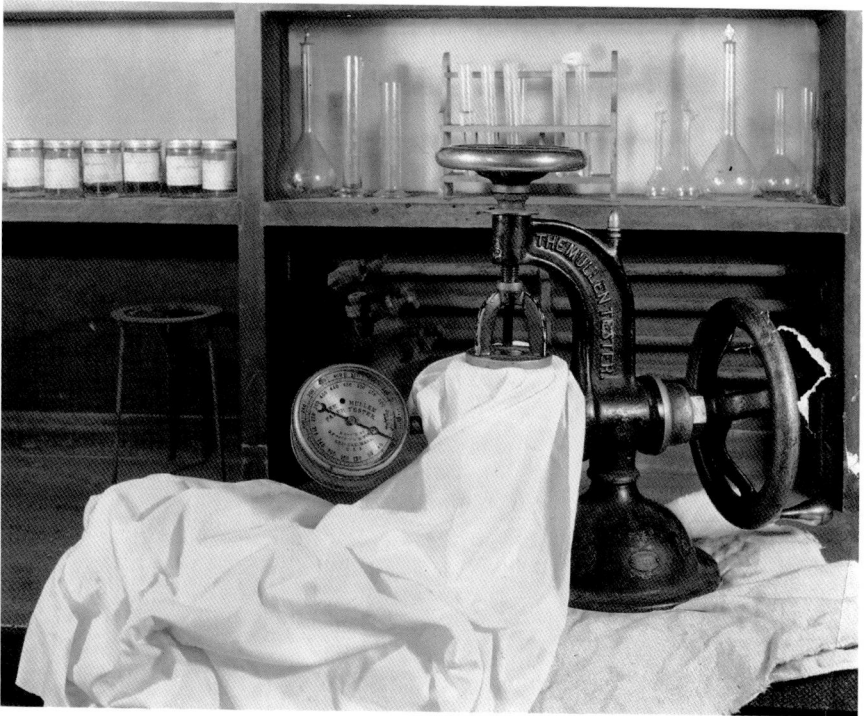

This machine is testing the performance of fabric used in store merchandise. The Kaufmann's fellowship provided the data to allow the store to choose the best materials for store-brand products. By the early 1930s, a team of 116 specialists had evaluated fifty-six different products.

found that two-thirds of the time, the customer had not followed usage instructions. The findings would be shared with the customer, but money was not returned.

The work was used to underscore claims of quality in advertisements and to provide better instructions for product usage. Employees were encouraged to tour the institute and share what they learned with customers. Customers were also encouraged to stop and ask the "Science-Service Girls" if they had shopping or product-care questions. The women, all home economists, were stationed in red booths in the downstairs store and on five selling floors. Customers could visit a laboratory on the sixth floor.

Kaufmann's developed a quality standards exhibit that traveled to stores in New Orleans, Miami and Washington, D.C., after debuting in Pittsburgh on November 19, 1934. It contrasted one hundred quality items with inferior merchandise—slips, panties, stockings, diapers, girl's dresses and more. For example, the evaluation of rayon, a new product, showed that the fabric was fragile when wet and encouraged home sewers to use ample seam allowance on rayon garments.

Driven by the economy, Kaufmann's, like other stores, turned away from high fashion as clothing became more casual. Higher import duties on French clothing made it too expensive for average consumers, so stores turned to American designers, who often had a Hollywood connection. Kaufmann's ads featured simple dresses made of cotton; rayon replaced more expensive silk.

The turn to American designers and American products was also plain in the housewares department. Modern designs prevailed. Sales of crystal and formal china dropped as women bought smaller sets of colorful china like Homer Laughlin's wildly popular Fiestaware. Department stores increased their share of the furniture market by selling colonial furniture by American manufacturers.

In spite of the economy, some Pittsburgh consumers could still indulge their expensive tastes, and Kaufmann's did not ignore them. E.J. believed that it was important to cater to Pittsburgh's different income levels with the basement and mid-level merchandise. He supported his wife, Liliane Kaufmann, when she suggested a high-end shop selling unique gifts and accessories called Vendome after the Place Vendome in Paris. Soon Vendome was selling "not fadd-y fashion" but quality clothing in a space that featured chrome, aspen wood and comfortable pastel chairs, all designed by Laszlo Garger, a Viennese decorator.

Vendome ads were small and discreet with simple fashion illustrations and often appeared on the society pages. Shoppers were advised that an express elevator would take them directly to the eleventh floor. In April 1934, Vendome advertised custom-made gloves, slips, blouses and shirts; that Christmas, it was taking orders for custom-made men's silk pajamas. Vendome was expanded in 1937 with a bigger space that included hats and shoes, as well as designer clothing.

In 1934, Liliane Kaufmann suggested opening an Elizabeth Arden salon to complement Vendome. The red door opened in January 1935. Advertising reassured women that they no longer had to travel to New York for beauty treatments or for fashion. They could simply take the express elevator to Kaufmann's eleventh floor.

Throughout the Depression, Kaufmann's continued its special events to draw people to the store. In March 1930, Miss Arnold, a former Ziegfeld girl, demonstrated the "Battle Creek Health Builder" home

During the Depression, sales of traditional fine china slumped, but shoppers bought smaller sets of colorful tableware. Popular Fiestaware, produced in the region, can be seen in this Kaufmann's display.

exercise machine. In March 1932, the store hosted an exhibit of Russian imperial items collected by the Hammer brothers. "Don't be wasteful of cosmetics, use them properly," encouraged a July 1934 presentation in the cosmetics department.

Hollywood celebrities often visited stores. In May 1935, Colleen Moore accompanied her doll house to Kaufmann's for an exhibit. "When I walked into Kaufmann's and saw that lovely first floor, the shining black columns, the beautiful murals, I—well, I just stood and stared." At a dinner for her, the actress autographed place cards for guests. Elizabeth Arden also visited the store that May.

In the following years, there was a Canary Circus, a costume show featuring thirty-four famous children from history and the world's largest model railroad, as well as regular author visits in the book department. Kaufmann's also used radio to attract shoppers. In 1930, the store sponsored a morning show on WJAS with two radio personalities—Dick Powell and

Bernie Armstrong—and "The Girl from Kaufmann's," who would describe products and events on the air. In 1932, "Babette," a local newspaper columnist, began a morning series of "household and style talks" sponsored by the store on WWSW.

In January 1934, Kaufmann's became the first store in the country to broadcast world news to the public. "Kaufmann's Breaks the News," hosted by Beckley Smith on WJAS, was part of Transradio News Service. News was presented in three fifteen-minute segments each day—at 12:30 p.m., 6:15 p.m. and 11:00 p.m.—and in news flashes throughout the day. When a New Jersey jury found Bruno Hauptman guilty in the Lindberg kidnapping, Kaufmann's broke the news on radio within minutes. The store also sponsored a *Woman's Digest Radio Program* each morning with Florance Sando and a sports program at 6:00 p.m. with Bob Prince.

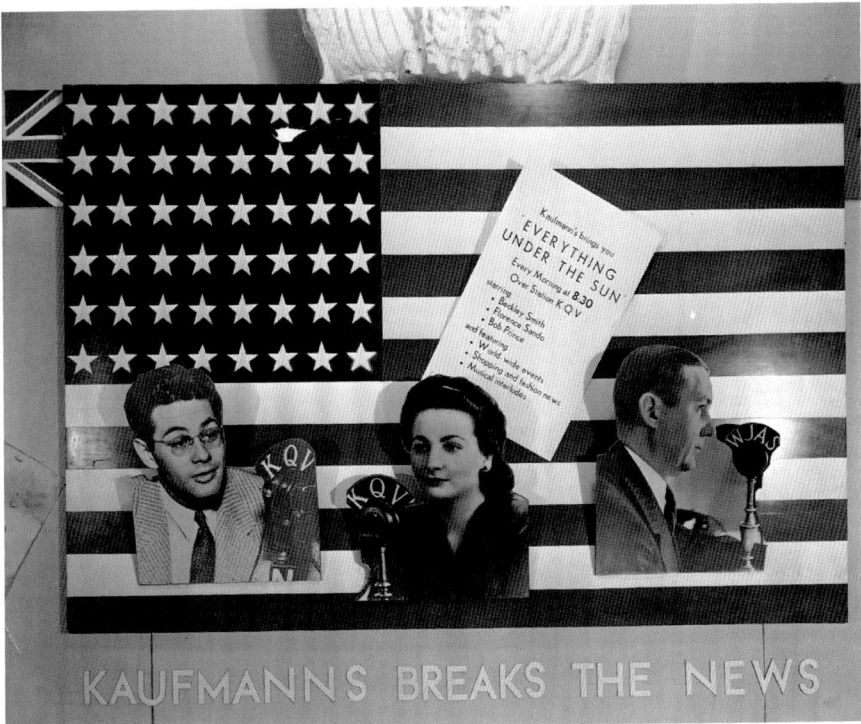

Kaufmann's adopted radio as a marketing tool in the early 1930s. The store sponsored a variety program with singer Dick Powell and the "Radio Girl" who told listeners about Kaufmann's products, sales and events. Later, the store sponsored a radio news program and a sports program with Bob Prince. Kaufmann's discontinued its radio programming in the 1950s when television became more popular.

In the summer of 1936, Kaufmann's began closing early on Saturdays in July and August, a move the employees appreciated. Ads announcing the move proclaimed, "Kaufmann's believes in the week-end," and included a ditty featuring the clock: "Hickory, dickory dock. This is the Kaufmann's clock. When the clock strikes one, it's time for FUN. Hickory, dickory, dock."

During the 1930s, Kaufmann's launched an annual anniversary sale, "The Month of Roses," with an emphasis on education over hard selling. An advertisement in 1931 emphasized science in support of retail and used the term "Peaks" in conjunction with the anniversary. By 1936, the concept had evolved into the "Peaks of Progress"; that year, "an epochal year of progress in the history of mankind," eleven stained-glass windows displayed in the store windows marked the "peaks" for the year, chosen by a jury of local historians.

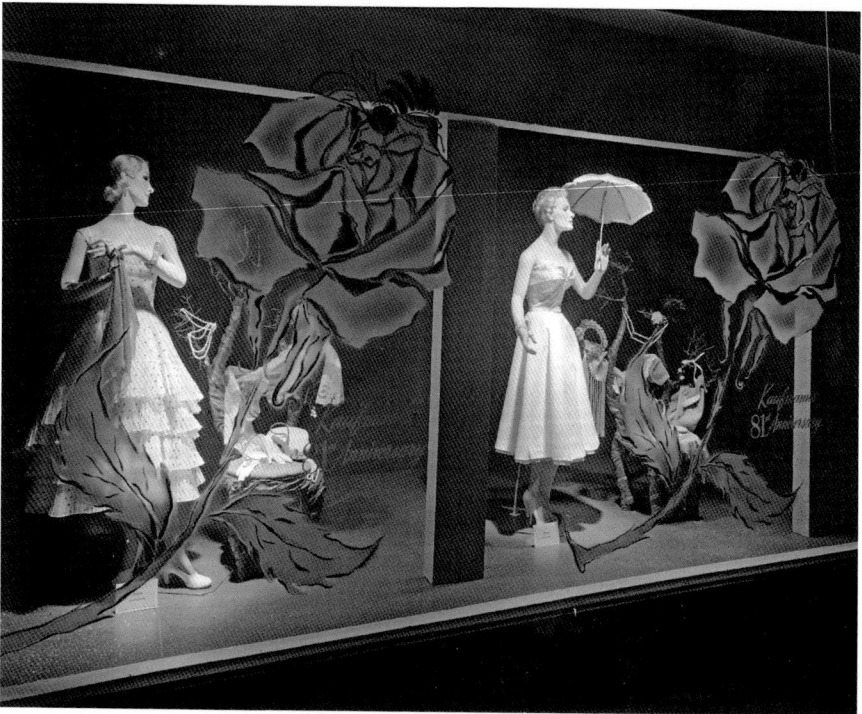

June was dubbed the "Month of Roses," and roses were a consistent anniversary theme as far back as the store's golden anniversary, when employees presented store management with a six-foot loving cup made of roses.

The store often looked back to its past for inspiration in celebrating anniversary events. Representing Kaufmann's early years, models in "historic" clothing and wigs pose for an anniversary event.

By 1939, the windows displaying the nine peaks were dedicated at a breakfast for local leaders. Contests for schoolchildren were also part of the celebration. The highlight of the event was Pittsburgh's first demonstration of television, with the mayor as the first on-air guest. The demonstration ran daily for two weeks, with broadcasts by local radio personalities in the eleventh-floor auditorium. RCA provided the television receivers.

Anniversary sales, launched with "Peaks of Progress" events, continued into the early war years. In 1940, Kaufmann's sixty-ninth anniversary, five windows were dedicated to the ten "Peaks," which included chemotherapy, synthetic fibers, rural electrification and new steel alloys. "Peaks" for 1941 included FM radio, synthetic rubber, new methods of blood transfusion and military defense.

By the late 1930s, the national economy was improving, and Kaufmann's advertising spoke to the rising prosperity. Furs and fashion were again featured in regular store advertising. In 1937, the store reported its highest sales and best stock performance since 1929. That fall, Kaufmann's held its first Career Women's Fashion Show and Dinner, an event that harkened back to the fashion events in the main store during the 1920s. It was so popular that it was repeated in the spring.

In March 1938, the store's board of directors elected Edgar Kaufmann Jr., E.J.'s only child, as secretary of the corporation and member of the board. He had served as assistant merchandising manager of the housewares department and on the store's buying staff in New York.

For Kaufmann's, the future looked brighter. But those perusing the French fashion that had returned to the store ads couldn't help but notice the stories and headlines on the same pages that reported worsening conditions in Europe and Asia.

Chapter 5

KAUFMANN'S GOES TO WAR

By 1940, the lean years of the Depression were coming to an end, and Kaufmann's had sold $2 million more in merchandise than it had in 1939. But news from Europe and Asia was distressing. War relief groups were meeting regularly in the store, and military motifs were appearing in fabric, clothing and cosmetics. By February 1941, the store was advertising fashion news from Los Angeles instead of Paris. In June, Kaufmann's hosted a Defense Show where visitors could see the latest military technology: the Garand rifle and "Blitz Buggy," an early version of the Jeep.

Kaufmann's had been through two other wars—the Spanish-American War in 1898 and World War I in 1917–18. During World War I, the store had actively supported Belgian war relief and had a Military Service Bureau on the eleventh floor where "all manner of foods, dainties, smokes, articles of clothing may be ordered at prevailing Paris prices for delivery to 'The Boy' anywhere in France."

World War II would prove much more challenging. Retailing was an essential industry during the war, and stores generally cooperated with the command economy dictated from Washington. People still shopped—right after Pearl Harbor, stores were crowded with people not just Christmas shopping but buying consumer goods that they thought might get scarce later.

The War Production Board (WPB), created in January 1942, rationed clothing and established regulations that drove fashion. The Office of Price Administration (OPA) regulated retail prices and store sales; price controls were introduced in April 1941. In 1943, the government banned the use of the word *sale* in advertising. The Treasury Department assigned monthly war bond quotas for stores to fulfill, and it had to adjust to much higher income and excess profit taxes.

With rationing and materials diverted to wartime industries, stores often had trouble getting merchandise to sell. A November 1944 profile of Kaufmann's in *Fortune* magazine included a long list of items the store could not stock. When employees left for the service or for jobs in war industries, stores introduced more self-service and discontinued other services in the name of patriotism.

Like many department stores, Kaufmann's supported the war effort. E.J. Kaufmann served as a "dollar-a-year" man with the OPA, and Irwin Wolf served on OPA's retail advisory committee. The store was fully compliant. Other members of the family were serving in the military—Oliver Kaufmann as a major in the air force and executive officer of an air field in Italy, and Edgar J. Kaufmann Jr. as a lieutenant in U.S. Army Air Forces Intelligence.

Kaufmann's employees were also in uniform; eventually, 450 former employees would be in the service. A *Storagram* poll early in the war asked employees, "What Can We Do for Our Service Men?" The six from the men's trousers department who were called up received wristwatches from co-workers; a man from draperies received a box with cigarettes, candy and cookies and a lighter at Christmas; and one section manager had his staff send cards and letters to former co-workers. Forty employees on the store's arcade floor bought defense bonds and stamps every Wednesday.

The store also supported its former employees, sending the *Storagram* and Christmas greetings to them. In late 1942, three hundred "Kaufmannites" in the service each received a ten-dollar money order. At eleven o'clock every morning, the entire store stopped working while the sixth-floor superintendent led a silent prayer for former employees and relatives in the service.

With 150 fewer employees during the war, Kaufmann's was forced to curtail some services, including wrapping and delivery. Shoppers were encouraged to take their packages with them. Early in the war, employee turnover was 10 percent, but this dropped to 5 percent after 1941, even though there were ample job opportunities in Pittsburgh's war industries. Managers noted that fewer employees did not mean a drop in service even during the Christmas rush.

There were other indications that the country and the store were at war. Kaufmann's developed an Air Raid Protection Program to safeguard customers, employees and merchandise in case of attack. At the alert signal—four long rings of a bell—air raid squads would escort co-workers and shoppers to one of the Safety Centers in the middle of the third through ninth floors. There, away from outside walls and windows, they would wait for the "all clear" signal—one long bell. The store also trained a first-aid squad for each floor and evacuation units for serious injuries. Department heads would direct salespeople to cover the merchandise before leaving the floor and to lock registers. Talented employees were asked to entertain those in the Safety Centers.

Four "roof watchers" were also assigned to stand on the roof and watch for incendiary bombs. These men wore helmets, gas masks, wool coats and

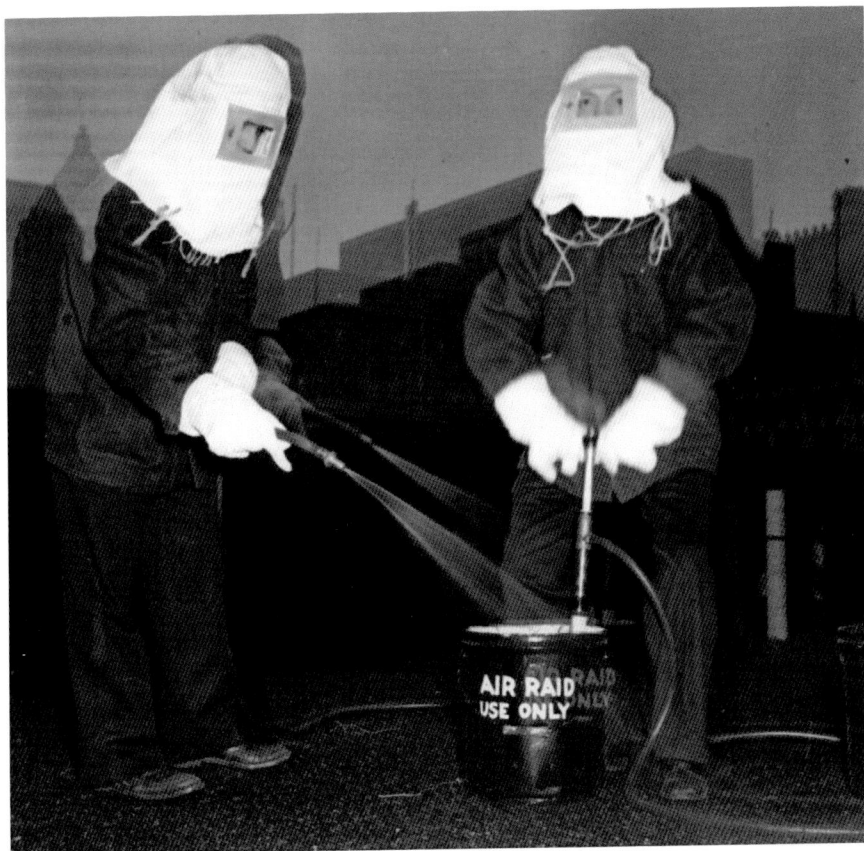

Kaufmann's prepared for potential air attacks in Pittsburgh with a complete air raid plan and store drills. The plan included air raid responders in heavy protective clothing who would go to the roof and put out incendiary bombs before they could set the store on fire.

KAUFMANNITES!
LET'S GO ALL-OUT
FOR VICTORY GARDENS!

STORAGRAM . PUBLISHED BY KAUFMANN'S EMPLOYEES . APRIL 1943

Kaufmann's encouraged the community
and its employees to support the war effort.
The store sold the supplies necessary to put
in and maintain victory gardens.

trousers, as well as heavy shoes and special gloves. They were provided with pumps, buckets, axes, shovels and sand to deal with bombs. The store had similar programs in place for its warehouses.

In February 1942, Kaufmann's was the first store in the country to plan furnishings for defense worker housing. As a model, designers used the Glen Hazel Housing Project, a new plan that housed one thousand families of Pittsburgh defense workers. The goal was to help defense workers live more comfortably as they put in long hours at critical industries. Four of the model rooms—a living room, master bedroom, a boy's room and a kitchen/dinette—were displayed in the store.

Kaufmann's set up a Serviceman's Gift Center and Victory Center where packages were mailed at no charge to servicemen. The store also established a dedicated shop, the Officer's Post, within the men's store that sold authorized army and navy uniforms and accessories. It provided a twenty-four-hour alteration service on emergency orders. Store advertisements noted that Kaufmann's Officer's Post had served a sixty-five-person hospital unit, officers from India and a navy ensign who needed to replace his uniform after surviving the sinking of his submarine. At Christmas 1943, pictures of war fronts were used in the window displays. The following spring, the twelve windows along Smithfield Street represented "neighbor nations," American allies throughout the world. A War Products Board exhibit on the ninth floor highlighted Pittsburgh's leading war industries, while more than 100,000 people attended an Army Show. Advertisements in the spring reminded shoppers that it was "Victory Garden Time."

The store also played a role in funding the war. In May 1941, advertisements reminded readers that "Kaufmann's is the first store in America to sell United States Defense Savings Stamps." The stamps, designed to help the government raise "the billions needed for National Defense," were sold in a special booth on the first floor.

Even before Pearl Harbor, Kaufmann's was promoting support of national defense. Windows were used to encourage civilian support, including volunteering and buying war bonds.

During World War II, Pittsburgh women as well as men worked in the local defense industries. This Kaufmann's window celebrates a familiar local scene: women doing what was previously men's work in a factory.

Once war had been declared, Kaufmann's continued to sell war stamps and war bonds. Special events encouraged the public to buy. For the Third War Loan Drive in September 1943, the store staged a huge street rally where a newscaster announced the Italian surrender. The original Norman Rockwell paintings of the "Four Freedoms" were on display, and everyone who bought a bond received reprints of the paintings. During the drive, Kaufmann's sold $7.5 million in Victory Bonds.

Early the next year, Kaufmann's sponsored a War Bond Show in the Syria Mosque that featured the original radio program *Quiz Kids*, including Pittsburgh kids who had appeared on the show. The show raised almost $5 million. Bond sales for the Fourth War Loan totaled $5,851,200. The store also raised money for the Red Cross War Fund by soliciting employees and holding a gala benefit. In addition, employees contributed more than $16,000 to the United War Fund for aid agencies in the United States and overseas.

These activities were part of the store's core values. As *Fortune* noted in a profile of E.J. Kaufmann, "He thinks his store has another distinction, and he is even more zealous about it—'Kaufmann's close identification with the community.' By ten-thirty on the morning of D-Day, for example, every Kaufmann billboard throughout the Pittsburgh area was covered with the words 'Kaufmann's joins the nation in prayer—God speed our boys.'"

In general Kaufmann's prospered during the war years. Rationed goods and some low-priced items were hard to get, but Irwin Wolf told *Fortune* that they didn't have problems dealing with manufacturers. He attributed that to the store's behavior twenty years earlier: in the 1921 collapse, Kaufmann's took a $750,000 loss on merchandise it had ordered in the boom, while most stores canceled their orders.

The *Storagram* also reported the store's success in keeping the shelves stocked in July 1945: "When President Harry S. Truman shopped his home town (Independence, Missouri) recently for white shirts and found none, Kaufmann's hearing of the President's predicament, immediately dispatched white shirts in the President's size to the White House. The Store was fortunate to have white shirts in the required size as Kaufmann's in common with other stores is not well stocked in white shirts."

By the "Month of Roses" in 1942, the United States was officially in the war, and the "Peaks" chosen that year did not represent the progress of man but rather the progress of the Allies against the Axis. Wendell Willkie spoke to breakfast attendees by phone from New York. That year, shortages also affected

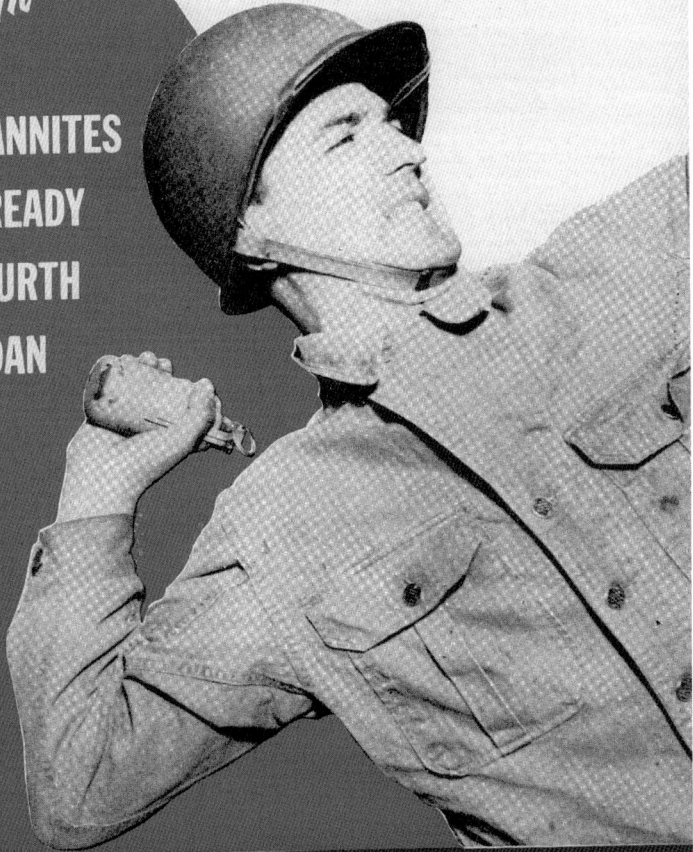

The Kaufmann's magazine, the *Storagram*, established in 1920, was sent to every store employee in the service. Hundreds of employees were either drafted or volunteered for service. Many of them returned to work in the store when they were discharged.

the annual anniversary sale, and Kaufmann's admitted that it was only able to offer sale prices because it had bought merchandise months before.

In 1943, "Peaks of Progress" continued its tradition, even though the anniversary sale was curtailed by government restrictions on sale pricing. Some departments were prohibited from participating in the sale, which only ran for two weeks. But there was a "Peaks" breakfast and a contest for students, and the windows on Smithfield Street highlighted Lend-Lease, air transportation, women in war and mass production.

Kaufmann's didn't even attempt to hold anniversary sales in June 1944 and 1945. Less than a week before the D-Day landings, advertisements encouraged people to stop at the store windows "[t]o see the ten vital reasons why America will win the war—and then the peace!" Among those ten were jet propulsion, radar, medical advances, PPG's bullet-resistant glass and labor-management cooperation. A one-acre exhibit on the ninth floor showed how management and labor in twenty-five Pittsburgh industries were cooperating in the war effort. Just weeks after the Germans had surrendered, the 1945 "Peaks" focused on postwar activities. That year, Kaufmann's displayed an exhibit of battlefield art.

Pittsburgh was a center of military manufacturing, and people had money to spend. Since they couldn't buy cars, they spent on jewelry and furs. The first floor was doing 60 percent more business, and people who had once shopped in the bargain basement had enough money to shop upstairs. Kaufmann's had 30 percent of the business done by the nine large department stores in the city. Sales rose from $25 million in 1939 to $35.5 million in 1943 and $37 million in 1944.

Although the country was still at war, there were some international sales. In June 1944, the *Storagram* reported that the watch repair department had received a package and letter from a soldier on the Anzio beachhead in Italy. He asked the craftsmen to repair his watch and wrote, "It may interest you to know that the enclosed Crawford was purchased at Kaufmann's shortly after I received my 'Greetings' which was over three years ago. I've given it a terrific beating since, but it had held up nobly. Return pronto, please, as I've grown rather attached to it—besides it used to tell time." The watch arrived in one piece, and the store repaired it.

The war also provided opportunities that would contribute to the postwar boom. The ChargaPlate technology emerged along with more flexible credit options. Shoppers liked increased self-service because they could browse without feeling pressure to buy. They embraced the new emphasis on sportswear, including pants for women. Telephone sales boomed.

And those on the front lines planned their store visits. In November 1944, the *Storagram* reported, "One of our customers tells us that she recently received a letter from her nephew, Sgt. George W. Potts, who is stationed on a lonely island in the Pacific. In the letter, he expresses nostalgic thoughts of home, and says that the first thing he will do when he gets back to Pittsburgh is come to Kaufmann's Restaurant and order a big batch of Aunt Mary's waffles!" Aunt Mary presided over the "Pancake Hut," where seventy-five cents could buy sausage, coffee and a choice of either corn, flannel or buckwheat pancakes.

In spite of the hardships of the Depression and the war, Kaufmann's future looked secure. As Irwin Wolf told *Fortune*, "There will always be department stores, and they will always be profitable."

Chapter 6

THE POSTWAR BOOM

With the end of World War II, Pittsburghers, like most Americans, were ready to shop, and Kaufmann's was ready to indulge them. After rationing, people had a pent-up desire for consumer goods, and young families were feathering their nests for the baby boom. A spirit of optimism and progress pervaded the country.

Kaufmann's Diamond Anniversary in 1946 was a yearlong event with fashion shows that debuted Dior's "New Look," a Rose Festival TV show and the first Civic Light Opera performance. The store also developed the Pittsburgh in Progress Plan and presented it to the community. And the sales were back: in advertisements, Kaufmann's claimed that it had $2 million more in merchandise than it usually stocked for anniversary sales.

Peaks of Progress kicked off the anniversary with a breakfast on June 1, broadcast on KDKA radio. Breakfast speaker Major General Curtis LeMay, discussing "The Army Air Force and Atomic Bomb Tests," declared, "The next war probably will start with bombs falling on Pittsburgh instead of Pearl Harbor." He encouraged scientific research and maintaining a strong defense to keep the nation safe.

In fashion, Dior's "New Look" symbolized the changes that were occurring. Dresses designed to save rationed fabric gave way to very full skirts and opulent designs. Kaufmann's fashionist, Eleanor Reamer Smith, wrote from Paris in March 1948, "The past three weeks have been completely enchanting! Never before have the Paris openings seemed so breathtaking, we're certainly going to look more feminine than in years.

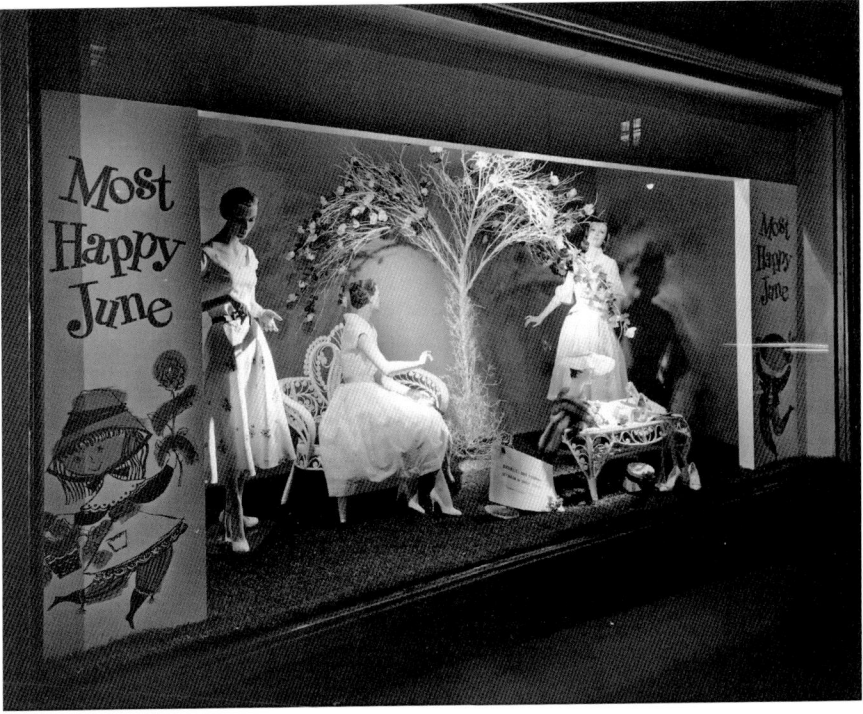

Anniversary sales were major events at Kaufmann's during the 1950s and 1960s. This window celebrates a "Most Happy June."

Like all good things you have to <u>see</u> them to believe how beautiful the new clothes are! Watch for them <u>first</u> at Kaufmann's. I'll let you know the minute they arrive."

Other changes would not bode well for the store. Edgar J. Kaufmann Jr., who had told *Fortune* that he was more interested in art than the department store business, left for a career in New York. In 1946, E.J. sold Kaufmann's to the May Company. The store retained its iconic name and eventually became the flagship store of a regional Kaufmann's Division.

The move also allowed E.J. to become more active in the community, particularly in Pittsburgh's urban renewal. As an active member of the Allegheny Conference on Community Development, he developed a planning document in 1946 that envisioned the new Pittsburgh. "Pittsburgh in Progress" introduced the idea of a Point Park and proposed redevelopment of the Lower Hill District with apartments and a cultural district. It also proposed relocating industry to reduce smoke and a sewage treatment plant to reduce river pollution.

Above: By the 1950s, June anniversary sales at Kaufmann's had become month-long events.

Opposite, top: Kaufmann's opened its Bridal Shop in 1947, in time for the marriage boom among returning veterans. Brides visited the store to buy the requisite china, silver and glass, as well as furniture, bedding and appliances.

Opposite, bottom: Delivery service was curtailed during World War II because of rationing. Even though delivery was costly, stores continued offering the service after World War II. This vehicle was painted in celebration of Kaufmann's Diamond Jubilee in 1946.

Urban renewal was not the only trend that would affect downtown stores like Kaufmann's by destroying city neighborhoods. Federal funds were available for highways to the booming new suburbs, where families were dependent on cars. Suburban lifestyles required more sportswear than fashion, and sportswear could be made cheaply and sold in discount stores.

These future challenges were not apparent during the postwar boom. In 1951, President Irwin Wolf told Kaufmann's buyers that he was "extremely optimistic about overall prospects for 1951." He cited the high employment and wages driven by the country's defense program and Kaufmann's rising share of Pittsburgh's department store business.

PRODUCTION OF POWER FROM ATOMIC ENERGY

Above: Beginning in the 1930s, the annual Peaks of Progress coincided with the June anniversary sale. A committee of prominent Pittsburghers chose the most important advances of the previous year as the Peaks of Progress. Store windows highlighted each "peak," like this one featuring atomic energy.

Left: The "New Look" in the 1950s required serious underpinnings. At the time, the Kaufmann's department that sold foundations was still called the Corset Department, the same name used when the department was established in the late nineteenth century.

This optimism and E.J.'s commitment to downtown drove a major expansion of the flagship store, even though it was already the largest department store in the tristate area. "Despite a trend toward suburban branch stores, Kaufmann's accepted the challenge of the Golden Triangle's rebirth."

In 1949, Kaufmann's purchased the nineteen-story Frick Annex Building and remodeled it for all the store's non-selling departments and services. Floor-to-floor "bridges" were built to connect the annex to the main store, and a larger receiving platform was added. This increased selling space in the main store and increased and centralized space for stock, an efficient upgrade. A single-unit air-conditioning system and new elevators were installed in 1951. The annex began operating in August 1952.

The store also bought the Carnegie Building next door, "a massive and solidly constructed building" and the world's first steel structure. Razing it took almost a year. It was replaced with a "modern, windowless, marble-front ten-story building" that had three stories underground. From the

Parking was always an issue in downtown shopping, particularly since suburban stores had large parking lots and shoppers could park for free. Kaufmann's provided parking to lure suburbanites to the city and offered free parking with purchases.

The historic Carnegie Building was demolished to make way for the expanded store. The first steel building, it was constructed as a demonstration of new structural steel technology and took almost a year to demolish.

third floor up, floors of the new addition were precisely aligned with those of the existing store, and twenty-four new escalators were installed. American Bridge Company provided three thousand tons of steel used in the construction. On the façade, a twenty-four-foot "K" in a circle of dots identified the building.

The existing store was also upgraded. The Art Deco columns from 1930 were covered with wood and pastel fabric—that fabric also covered the elevator banks. New fixtures blended with the modern décor of the addition. Throughout the store, seventy-five pastel park benches reminded people to "Shop and Relax at Kaufmann's."

The expansion increased the selling space from 753,505 square feet to 1,158,852 square feet. While the store created few new departments, it did analyze sales results to assign new selling spaces and established some individual shops like the Clay Poole Shop for men. The toy department was given enough space that it didn't need to be moved for the holidays.

U.S. Steel supplied the beams used in construction of the 1955 Kaufmann's addition. Representatives from the store and U.S. Steel posed atop the steel skeleton.

Merchandising people teamed with display people to design individual departments, often using symbols to define spaces.

The new furniture department typified the changes. Furniture was selling well at the time, and Kaufmann's dedicated more than an acre of space to it. Furniture was shown in room groupings, a departure from "model rooms" with such impressive décor that they distracted shoppers from the furniture. The department also sold lighting and pictures, as well as "good, sound, well-designed, long-service furniture," and featured American-made pieces by Baker, Herman Miller and Kittinger. It also set up a Home Planning Center in the new space.

A major yearlong strike of delivery drivers proved only a minor nuisance during construction as both shoppers and clerks crossed picket lines. There was little public sympathy or support for the drivers, and their national headquarters, the International Teamsters, did not sanction it. Delivery costs in Pittsburgh were already twice as high as in other cities, and the local

The 1955 Kaufmann's addition was modern and faced with white marble. To save energy and optimize selling space, the only windows were the display windows on the ground floor.

press editorialized that lazy drivers cost both stores and consumers money. When the strike against Kaufmann's and four other Pittsburgh department stores ended, almost no one noticed.

Kaufmann's store expansion took three years. When it was finally completed, the store held an Open House Week for the public. It was launched with a Sunday evening cocktail party, where guests were greeted by models wearing fashions from 1871. During the week, there were continual informal fashion shows, demonstrations and special events; twenty-six original Grandma Moses paintings were on display, an English botanist arranged plastic flowers, the Maidenform Dream Girl visited the store and there were demonstrations of power tools and the Noodlemaker, a pasta

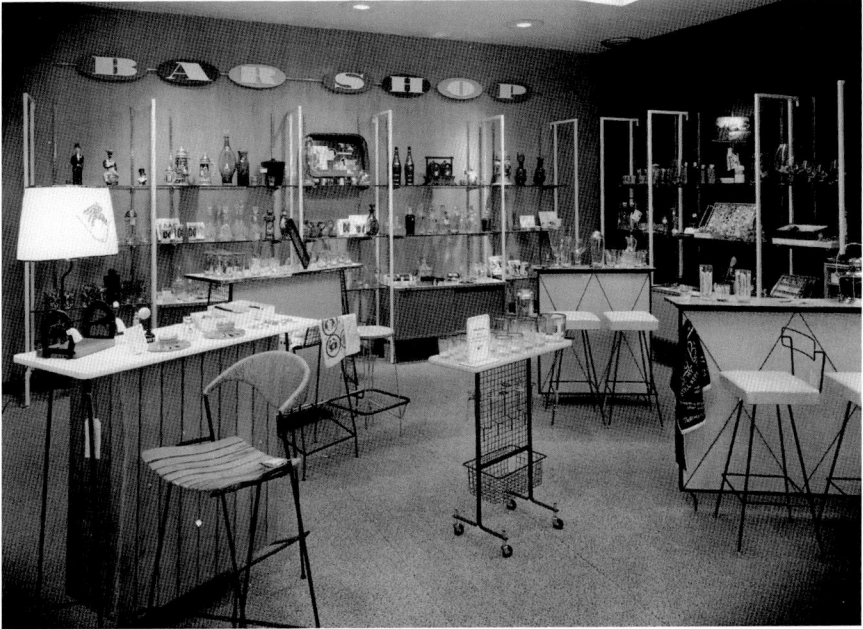

After the 1955 expansion, individual shops throughout the store were updated with modern décor. The Bar Shop took advantage of the era's interest in serving cocktails at home.

An expanded toy department catered to the children of the baby boom. By the 1950s, Kaufmann's was carrying national brand-name toys instead of the European imports that it had sold early in the century.

machine. At a Tinkerbell Party, Marty Wolfson of KDKA-TV and Josie Carey of WQED entertained the girls.

"Kaufmann's faith in Downtown Pittsburgh's renaissance program has been amply supported by completion of the store's 12 million-dollar expansion project," the marketing department wrote and noted that the store was largest shopping center between New York and Chicago.

The expansion created the Kaufmann's that generations of shoppers would know and love. Sadly, one person who had led the store through the challenges of the Depression and World War II was not at the opening. E.J. Kaufmann had died suddenly in his sleep on April 15, 1955, at his winter home in Palm Springs, California. Liliane had died three years earlier. Employees of the store, including more than seven hundred members of the Stand-By Club, were shocked, citing E.J.'s energy and ongoing work at the store. The Pittsburgh community was shocked, too, and newspapers were filled with condolence messages from civic leaders across the region.

Kaufmann's children's clothing departments often included elaborate imported clothing and special dresses for parties or holidays, like this display during the 1955 expansion. Departments were segregated by age and gender to increase sales.

College students became an important market segment in the 1940s. The 1955 Kaufmann's store expansion included a college shop.

With fourteen selling floors, Kaufmann's was billed as the "Most Complete Shopping Center Anywhere" and the "Fashion Point of the Golden Triangle." As the *Storagram* reported, "Branch Rickey of the Pittsburgh Pirates wanted a left-handed catcher, an unheard of thing in baseball and could not find a left-handed glove anywhere. Dave Grossman our Sporting Goods buyer opened a drawer and pulled out a glove and shipped it to Rickey with Kaufmann's compliments."

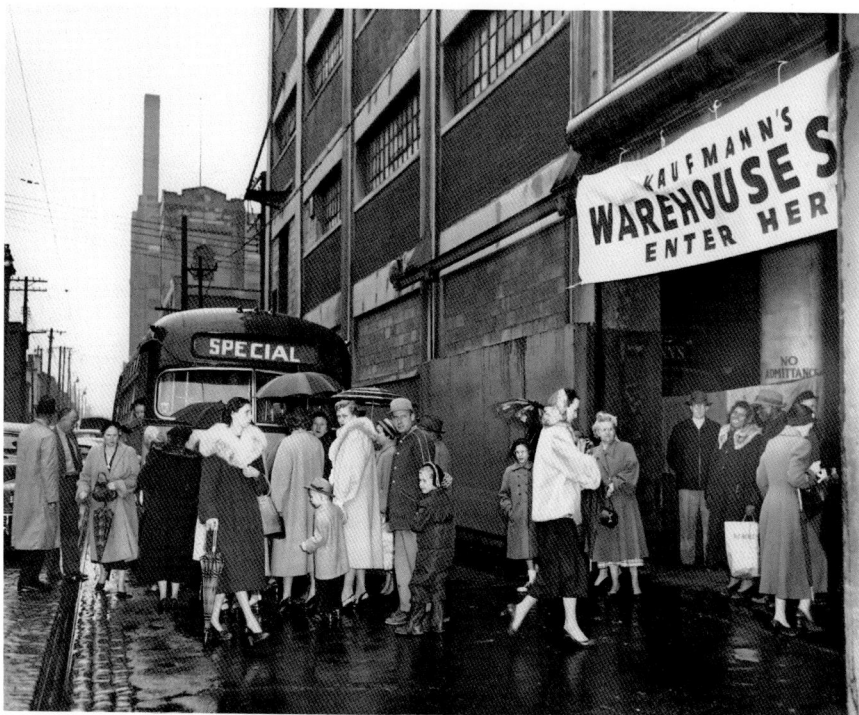

Warehouse sales were first held in the 1940s and were popular during the 1950s and 1960s. Shoppers could find bargains in furniture and appliances.

For those who couldn't come into town, there was phone shopping: "[W]hen bad weather, family illness, or just household chores keep you at home, just call…to put all of Kaufmann's vast facilities at your beck and call…from face cream to refrigerators…Call Grant 1-7000…Our new order board makes shopping at home easier than ever." Sixty phone clerks who could take ten thousand orders each day would "speed" them by pneumatic tube to the proper departments, where orders would be filled within thirty minutes.

Phone shopping was just one service that Kaufmann's offered. Shoppers could arrange travel, buy concert tickets, take driver training, fill prescriptions, post a letter, plan a wedding and order custom slipcovers or awnings. There was a barbershop and three different beauty salons for different budgets. The store could also clean and repair furs and gloves and repair sewing machines, cameras, radios and fountain pens.

Lunch was always an integral part of the downtown shopping experience, and Kaufmann's introduced a new option in its expanded store: the Tic

Toc Restaurant, which opened on March 21, 1953. It not only appealed to shoppers but also drew office workers from downtown corporations. Diners quickly developed favorites that stayed on the menu for decades, including the Original Tic-Toc Burger, the Reuben and the Tic Toc Tea Plate—tea sandwiches that came with a choice of chicken or gelatin salad. The desserts were legendary; made on the premises, they included pecan balls, cakes and Mile High Ice Cream Pie.

The store also operated the Arcade Tea Room and adjoining restaurant on the eleventh floor that served 3,500 to 4,000 people each day. The two had the largest combined capacity in the city, and many on the staff had worked there for decades. Huge commercial dishwashers cleaned 10,000 pieces of china, 5,000 pieces of silverware and 2,500 glasses each day. For years, Kaufmann's restaurants were listed in the Duncan Hines book *Better Places for Eating*.

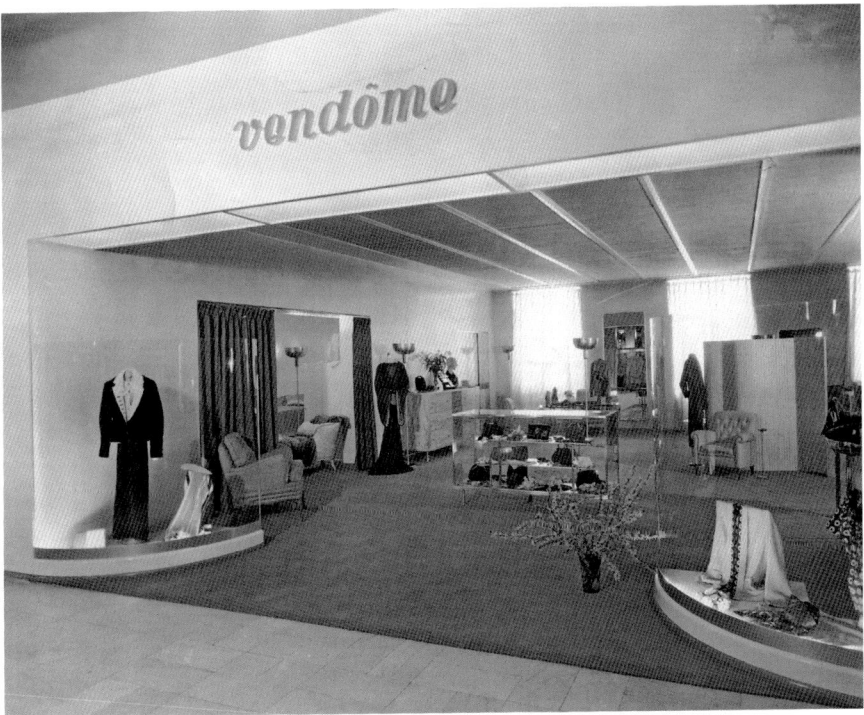

The Vendôme Shop catered to high-end shoppers who could take an express elevator to its location on the eleventh floor. The shop specialized in clothing from French and Italian designers.

The Elizabeth Arden Beauty Shop was close to the Vendôme on the eleventh floor. Kaufmann's had multiple salons in the store to cater to customers' different budgets.

Desserts from the restaurant were sold in the store's Arcade Bakery. They were created by a Kaufmann's pastry chef, whose staff baked hundreds of pies and cakes each day. Kaufmann's also made all of its own ice cream.

Entertainment and educational events continued in the expanded store. In October 1951, 250,000 people visited Kaufmann's Italian Fair, where

Kaufmann's provided dozens of repair and maintenance services in addition to selling new merchandise. Here specialists use sawdust to clean furs in the 1950s; the store also provided fur repair and storage.

they bought seven thousand pounds of imported cheese and enough salami to reach from the store to the Point if laid end to end. The dining room served one thousand spaghetti dinners, and a 1:100 scale replica of St. Peter's—more than fifteen feet long—was on display.

For a California show in 1953, the store exhibited twenty-one models of Spanish missions and imported two tons of desert sand and 750 plants to re-create a desert scene at night. There were California foods with Spanish and Oriental influences. The Smithfield Street windows were transformed into California market scenes.

One of Kaufmann's most ambitious events was "Steelaire Fifth Avenue," also known as the "House on the Roof" in August 1957. A prefab steel house, it had seven rooms and exterior glass walls, covered 1,500 square feet and used six tons of steel. Kaufmann's decorated and furnished the interior, landscaped the exterior and had a 1909 Stanley Steamer hoisted to the roof for the carport. U.S. Steel, producer of the Steelaire, and several gas companies collaborated on the project. Mrs. America greeted visitors—sixty thousand by September—in the all-gas kitchen. It was, the press reported, "like a transplanted bit of suburbia" on top of Kaufmann's new addition.

Four years later, a second house—this one a larger split level—was constructed. Kaufmann's teamed with builder Edward M. Ryan and several gas companies to build a three-bedroom, two-and-a-half-bath house with a gravel driveway, a lawn and a swimming pool. Water in the pool was only four inches deep because of weight limitations.

In two months, 110,000 people traveled downtown to visit Kaufmann's roof. But they didn't need to. Nine identical houses were located in new housing plans in the suburbs east, south and north of the city. The goal of the entire project was to stimulate home building. It was a success. Kaufmann's would soon build suburban branches in three of the suburbs where the models were located.

Chapter 7

CHRISTMAS AT KAUFMANN'S

Holidays were big business for department stores. While we associate the stores with Christmas, other holidays often got more attention in the late nineteenth century. Stores held grand spring openings, often at Easter, with the new season's clothing. A few decades after the Civil War, Decoration Day (now Memorial Day) was marked with parades and picnics. Kaufmann's advertised Grand Army of the Republic (GAR) uniforms for the big day, with moveable buttons to accommodate the increasing bulk of old soldiers in the veterans organization.

By the mid-1880s, Kaufmann's was including Christmas goods in its regular advertisements and had started two holiday traditions. Santa appeared at the store in the "Mammoth Corner Window" in 1883, and the store began distributing Christmas books to local Sunday schools in 1885.

In 1885, the mammoth window was transformed into Fairyland, and Santa appeared in "Regal Magnificence." The next year, store advertisements showed Santa arriving at Kaufmann's in a ship with "holiday goods." The window was now "Kris Kringles's Ice Palace," but Santa also held court in the boys' department. In 1889, he brought with him a "Pop Corn Bakery," and each visiting child got a popcorn ball. By the end of the decade, Santa's appearance had become a store tradition.

Another early Kaufmann's tradition was its distribution of Christmas readers to Sunday schools in Pittsburgh, Allegheny and surrounding counties. The first year, the store distributed 40,000 books; by 1897, it was distributing 100,000. As the press noted in 1889, it took twelve men a week

By the early twentieth century, Christmas shopping had become a yearly tradition.

Kaufmann's Christmas windows often featured cartoon characters that were popular at the time. In this window from the 1930s, Barney Google appears with his racehorse, Spark Plug.

to deliver the books, which had cost thousands of dollars, but while the gifts were generous, they were also given quietly. In December 1892, the year of the infamous steel strike, the children of Homestead received one pound of candy in addition to the books.

While the readers were sent to more than two hundred churches of many denominations for children in their Sunday schools, the content was not religious. A *Pittsburgh Magazine* writer described two of the books from 1905 and 1907: "There are silly bears on toboggans and a beautifully drawn chimpanzee photographer taking pictures of a well-dressed family of Victorian hippos! A two-cookie robbery in Snowbirdville is the subject of another cartoon.… One of the booklets has a children's adaptation of Charles Dickens' A Christmas Carol."

Kaufmann's began distributing picture books at Christmas in the late nineteenth century. The books did not contain religious content but were distributed by churches of many denominations throughout the Pittsburgh region. Clergy could contact the store and be placed on the distribution list.

By the end of the nineteenth century, Christmas had become a major Kaufmann's holiday. Store interiors were decorated; in 1894, five silver arches hung with gifts spanned the main aisle from the Fifth Avenue entrance. Pillars had been transformed into pine trees hung with ornaments and more gifts. Two years later, the store ran a two-page Christmas ad in the Sunday paper, and on Monday, so many shoppers flocked to Kaufmann's that it took a wagon to carry the day's proceeds to Farmers National Bank. The bank noted that it was the biggest one-day retail deposit ever: $72,177.96.

By 1910, Kaufmann's was billing itself as "Pittsburg's Christmas Store" with "acres of floorspace…miles of aisles." Shoppers were advised that waiting rooms, check rooms for parcels, restaurants and three thousand trained employees would make Christmas shopping easy and enjoyable. Santa figured prominently in ads, carrying hockey skates, men's shirts, handkerchiefs and toys.

SUNDAY SCHOOL
GREETINGS

KAUFMANN'S
THE BIG STORE
PITTSBURGH, PA.

By 1897, Kaufmann's was distributing 100,000 books to Pittsburgh churches at Christmas. In 1889, it took twelve men a week to complete the deliveries. The holiday tradition continued into the early twentieth century.

And toys were now central to Christmas, gathered at Kaufmann's in a special Toyland. In 1910, ninety-eight cents would buy an iron fire engine, imported doll, toy grocery store, soldier outfit, air rifle or tool chest. When the store was expanded, there was more room for Toyland; advertisements encouraged shoppers to "take the moving stairway to Toyland" on the fifth floor. There they would find a "block-long and block-wide land of joy...presided over by a Real Live Santa Claus." All children visiting Santa with an adult would receive a picture puzzle. Hot toys that year included a cinematograph moving picture machine, mechanical train sets and a teddy bear on wheels.

Kaufmann's Christmas became more sophisticated in the 1920s. A new display department decorated the first floor, and the *Storagram* exclaimed, "White Christmas Trees! Ever hear of them? Neither did we until Mr. Katz placed them all over the First Floor for the holiday decorations. Stunning is no word for the effect he had achieved."

Santa returned to Toyland, now filled with more expensive toys as parents had money to spend. A fire truck cost $3.50, a bisque-headed baby doll $4.95 and train sets from $6.95 to $8.50. Name-brand toys like the Bye-Lo Baby were also appearing.

The economic downturn of the 1930s strained family budgets, but Kaufmann's continued its Christmas traditions. The store advertised Christmas sales and Christmas merchandise, decorated windows and hosted Santa in Toyland. By 1933, it had adopted the slogan "Kaufmann's for everything under the tree," which it would use for several decades.

Others were joining Santa in Toyland, now a major installation on the ninth floor. Harry the Clown and his puppet show became a regular feature. Train sets had evolved into a large Lionel Train Center. In 1938, Toyland became the "World's Fair of Toys," and Disney's World's Fair show—with

Toyland had become a Christmas institution by the 1920s. Parents had money to spend and indulged their children with Christmas toys.

Bye-Lo Babies arrive at the store via stork during the International Exposition of Arts and Industries. By the 1920s, Kaufmann's was carrying national brands in its stores. Bye-Lo Babies, designed by Grace Putnam, were one of the first realistic baby dolls.

Mickey, Donald, the Seven Dwarfs and Ferdinand the Bull—was featured in Kaufmann's windows, along with a "real snow storm."

Children weren't the only recipients of toys. In 1938, Kaufmann's also had a Christmas Dog Shop with dog beds, dishes, coats and leads. For one dollar, shoppers could buy a dog stocking with four whistling rubber toys, a real bone and a box of dog candy.

War dominated Christmas celebrations in the 1940s. In December 1941, just after Pearl Harbor, Kaufmann's Christmas windows, "Toyland Prepares for Defense," culminated in an elaborate military wedding of the Painted Doll and Wooden Soldier. The windows, built in New York months before, were animated from 8:30 a.m. until midnight and all day Sunday. They attracted so much attention that people stood four deep on the side walk to watch them, and Kaufmann's doorman estimated that thirty-seven thousand people stopped each day.

That year, Toyland was again described as "a city block of toys." Santa returned with Harry the Clown, and the space on the ninth floor was

During World War II, Christmas windows reflected the reality of war. Window designers used different wartime themes. Here soldiers celebrate the holiday on various war fronts.

Christmas windows also promoted friendship with America's wartime allies. This holiday window shows Russian soldiers (far left) celebrating the holiday.

decorated as Fairyland. Disney's flying elephant Dumbo appeared with his mother, Jumbo. Store advertisements showed lots of military toys even before war was declared.

One year later, Kaufmann's advertised its evening shopping hours for defense workers and its services that made shopping more convenient. "Santa Belles" and "Santa Beaux" throughout the store would help customers with their shopping challenges. The belles wore red dirndls and green knit hats with bells, while the men wore gray slacks and green jackets. At the store's Victory Center, shoppers could find gifts for servicemen, WAACs, WAVES and nurses or buy the "best gift of all": a war bond. In Kaufmann's Hide Away Shop, a Santa Belle would help men "pick gifts of intimate apparel with nary a blush."

With the end of the war and pent-up demand, Christmas developed into a full-blown spending orgy. In 1947, using the theme "If it's out of this world— it's here," Kaufmann's advertised a special gift shop with European items that hadn't been available during the war. Imported children's clothing from France,

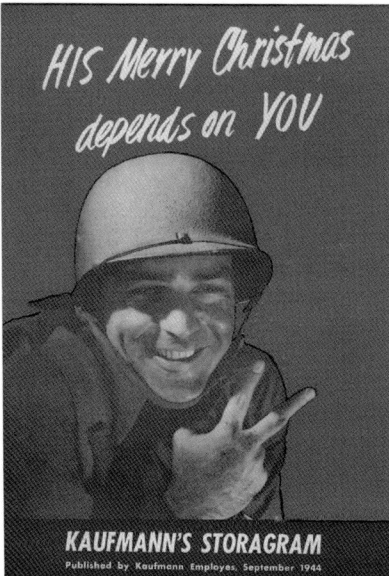

HIS Merry Christmas depends on YOU

KAUFMANN'S STORAGRAM
Published by Kaufmann Employes. September 1944

During World War II, shoppers at Kaufmann's Victory Center could find gifts for servicemen, WAACs, WAVES and nurses or buy the "best gift of all": a war bond.

Switzerland, England and Belgium was sold at holiday prices. The window displays that year had been made in Hollywood and featured an animated family that dreamed of Christmas. Of course, Santa was back in Toyland.

Santa was the star of Kaufmann's 1948 windows, where his life was celebrated in twenty-six "festive scenes." "Christmas just wouldn't be Christmas [...] without a visit to Kaufmann's windows," the store declared.

By 1955, Kaufmann's was offering the "Biggest Christmas in Town," with endless gift choices under one roof, "Clever Santa Belles" who would shop with you and 7,800 parking spaces within a few steps for those driving in from suburbia. In Toyland, Santa ruled a space "greater and more glorious than ever." In the 1955 store expansion, a large toy department had been permanently established on the ninth floor.

Planning for Christmas took store decorators six months to coordinate exterior décor, decorations in every department and the five traditional mechanical windows on Smithfield Street. In 1956, six thirty-foot live trees were set up in four hundred pounds of sand (for stability) on the marquees at the store entrances. They were decorated with red lights and topped with three-foot lighted white stars. The lights went on Monday, November 19, during Pittsburgh's Preview of Christmas. That year, the windows were themed "Christmas in Our Town" and included a firehouse, pet shop, floral shop, church, school and houses. Santa and the reindeer flew over several of the houses.

Kaufmann's was a Christmas shopping mecca in the 1960s. In addition to the 220 regular departments in the store, 21 special holiday boutiques focused on gifts. There was a "Christmas Idea Shop" in the fabric department for those who made their own gifts, "Sparkling Candle Bar" and "Trim the Home Shop" for décor and bars that sold aprons and slippers. Christmas windows featured characters from nursery rhymes.

Kaufmann's introduced "Santa Belles," who would assist Christmas shoppers in the 1940s. Here a "Santa Belle" from the 1960s helps a shopper.

On the ninth floor next to Toyland, Kaufmann's set up the "Children's Very Own Shop," a tradition that many adults remembered as their first department store shopping experience. There they could "buy for others…at piggy bank prices." No adults were allowed, so children could shop in "grown-up privacy." Children could also breakfast with Santa in Kaufmann's restaurant.

for
everything
under
the
tree

KAUFMANN'S .. Christmas 1961
DOWNTOWN   MONROEVILLE

"Kaufmann's for everything under the tree." By the 1960s, Kaufmann's Christmas traditions—Santa, animated windows and ornate decorations—were part of Pittsburgh's holiday celebrations. In 1961, children could shop for gifts for others in the Children's Own Gift Shop.

And the hot gift in the 1960s? Television. One advertisement encouraged shoppers to consider a twenty-three-inch Zenith Console TV. "Imagine this under the tree... spotlight dial, built-in antenna add more luxury...Just charge it." For those who wanted a color TV, Kaufmann's had the latest technology, and a liberal TV trade-in policy made buying easier.

The holiday boutique concept continued into the 1970s with shops tuned to the times: bar shop, toiletry bar and small gifts. Santa arrived by antique car. Kaufmann's windows featured *Sesame Street* characters, and the store introduced a new feature: the Talking Christmas Tree, a person in a large Christmas tree costume who bantered with customers.

Most holiday activities centered on the flagship store downtown, but suburban stores mirrored downtown traditions. Santa reigned in suburbia, where children could visit him and the Talking Christmas Tree. Most merchandise advertised downtown was also available in suburbia.

For suburbanites who ventured downtown, Kaufmann's provided perks—three hours of free parking for a five-dollar purchase, expanded evening hours and dinner in the restaurant. A Skywalk constructed over Forbes Avenue from the third floor of the store to the parking garage made parking more accessible.

The energy crisis of the 1970s dimmed the holiday. The lights encircling the "K" outside the store were turned off to save energy. Inflation, recession and collapse of the steel industry also challenged the store.

In 1981, Kaufmann's partnered with the city of Pittsburgh in what would become the store's last surviving tradition, the "Celebrate the Season" parade. Held downtown on the Saturday after Thanksgiving, it officially kicked off the holiday shopping season. The first year, the parade featured

While many Christmas activities, like animated windows and holiday parades, were centered downtown, suburban stores were also decorated for Christmas, and Santa held court in the toy department.

Santa was a perennial favorite in Christmas windows. He first appeared at Kaufmann's in the late nineteenth century, where he took up residence in one of Kaufmann's windows. At the time, the department store Santa was a new holiday feature.

local high school bands, the Pirate Parrot, Steelers players and local TV and radio personalities, as well as Santa and Mrs. Claus and the cast of *Mister Rogers' Neighborhood*.

Over the years, downtown economic development groups, local media, dozens of regional organizations and the general public supported the parade. When Kaufmann's became Macy's in 2006, the parade lived on, as did other Kaufmann's holiday traditions like breakfast with Santa and the Children's Own Shop. In 2014, Macy's stopped sponsoring the parade, although it assured Pittsburghers that other traditions would remain, like the animated windows.

Those windows outlived both Kaufmann's and Macy's. After the flagship store was shuttered in 2015, the new owner, with local funding, continued a Light Up Night tradition. When the window curtains opened, they revealed two historic Macy's windows and seven holiday windows decorated by local cultural institutions.

Chapter 8

WORKING AT THE BIG STORE

or many Pittsburghers, Kaufmann's was a great place to shop. For others, it was a great place to work. In the earliest days, the four brothers ran the store themselves, but as business prospered, they hired clerks, as well as tailors who made much of the clothing that they sold.

As the store expanded, so did opportunities for employment. Before child labor laws were passed, young teenagers could join the store as office boys, delivery helpers or "cash" boys or girls. Clerks did not handle money. Instead, a boy or girl would take the payment and literally run to the cashier's office and run back with the change. Workers who joined the store as children could rise through the ranks, becoming clerks, buyers or department heads. At the time, there was no formal application process. Nettie McKenzie, who spent her entire career at the store, remembered meeting with Henry Kaufmann on a Friday and starting the next day as a clerk in the millinery department.

Clerking was not a job with status; it ranked just above domestic or factory work, and many clerks came from the working classes. Until the Depression, middle- or upper-class women wouldn't dream of clerking in a department store. Men with college degrees rarely entered the field before the 1920s.

The status of clerks rose as more high school graduates became interested in retail and saw the position as a steppingstone to the coveted job of buyer. Ivy League schools began offering courses in department store management. By 1927, the local press was noting that Kaufmann's employment manager was glad to interview high school and college graduates for work. Fifty years later, the store was actively recruiting college graduates and had established training programs to prepare them for retail management careers.

Clerking was the most recognizable department store job, but it took more than clerks and managers to operate a large store. On the selling side were the buyers and department managers and their assistants. Supporting them were wrappers, packers and delivery people—shoppers rarely took packages home with them. There were stable workers, drivers and mechanics who kept wagons and trucks on the road and warehouse staff to load the trucks. The store ran a print shop and shops to repair furniture, carpets and awnings. It provided food service and offered alterations and custom clothing. All of these employed skilled craftspeople.

Advertising and promotion was done in house, providing jobs for fashion and events coordinators, artists, photographers and copywriters. Decorators

Above: Kaufmann's bought a second warehouse in 1913 to provide more space for furniture. The building, on a rail line for direct delivery, provided three and a half acres of floor space. It also included room for workshops. Here warehouse workers prepare an icebox for delivery in 1927.

Opposite, top: As a full-service store, Kaufmann's provided many jobs other than sales. These employees worked in the store's print shop.

Opposite, bottom: Kaufmann's maintained its own in-house print shop for signage and marketing materials. The print shop was located in the North Side warehouse.

Above: Kaufmann's food service workers worked in the store restaurants, cooked for the employee cafeteria and baked for the store bakery. Many worked at the store for decades. In the 1920s, Kaufmann's began hiring college-trained dieticians to manage their food services. The woman in the dark dress in this photo may have been the dietician.

Opposite, top: Kaufmann's telephone order department could field ten thousand calls per day. "Call Grant 1-7000.... Our new order board makes shopping at home easier than ever."

Opposite, bottom: Catalogues sent through the mail encouraged mail order. Kaufmann's had accepted mail-order sales from its earliest days, when it issued a *Fashion Journal* with complete instructions for providing measurements to the store's tailors.

designed windows and interior displays. The store provided its own credit cards; a large credit department managed the accounts. Kaufmann's also encouraged telephone shopping, and dedicated clerks answered the phones. It had its own security force, full engineering and maintenance staff and administrative people to handle the paperwork.

By the late 1920s, Kaufmann's employed several thousand Pittsburghers. In the late nineteenth and early twentieth centuries, department store work was grueling. Clerks often worked ten- to sixteen-hour days during the week and on Sundays and holidays, and sixty-hour workweeks were common.

(One early store ad reminded shoppers that the store would be closing at noon—on Christmas Day.) In October 1903, Kaufmann's announced that it was closing on Saturday at 6:30 p.m., a move that was popular with employees. The store had been open until 10:00 p.m. for thousands of late evening shoppers.

Pay for clerks was low, and there was no overtime; benefits were nonexistent. Perhaps because they had worked in the store with their employees, the Kaufmann brothers instituted or embraced improvements in working conditions. The store was closed on Sundays. In the 1930s, it closed at noon on summer Saturdays so employees could enjoy "the weekend." When the forty-hour week was mandated in the 1940s, Kaufmann's was one of the first stores in the country to institute the change. But there were caveats: in 1943, store policies required longer hours for six weeks during the year, and managers worked forty-eight-hour weeks. Overtime was discouraged since the store paid time plus one-third for it. (Kaufmann's also gave each employee a week of vacation in the first work year and two weeks after a year of work.)

Gertrude Gordon described how work at the store changed over the years in a 1920s *Storagram* article. A feature writer for the local press, she had been sent to the store on an undercover assignment. As she noted, it wasn't her first time working for Kaufmann's. She had first worked in the store as a fifteen-year-old temp, later returning as a demonstrator in the grocery department. In 1907, she left Kaufmann's to start her journalism career.

When she was hired as a teenager, she was just given a locker key and a scrap of paper with the name of the floor walker to whom she would report. Her fellow workers showed her how to do her job. They often worked until 10:00 p.m. on Saturdays and in the holiday rush. The women's restroom was small and uncomfortable; the only chairs were brought up from the shoe department. The employee's dining room was unattractive.

When she returned as a journalist/clerk twenty-five years later, she had to fill out an employment application and take several tests, including a "mental test," before she was assigned to the glove department. Before hitting the floor, she and twenty-five other new employees were given a store orientation presentation and several hours of training. And while the job itself involved standing for thirteen hours, she was impressed by upgrades in the restrooms and employee cafeteria. Kaufmann's seemed to consider employees as part of an extended family—the Kaufmannites.

In 1903, the store established the Employees' Benefit and Protective Organization, a mutual aid society. Open to all employees who had passed

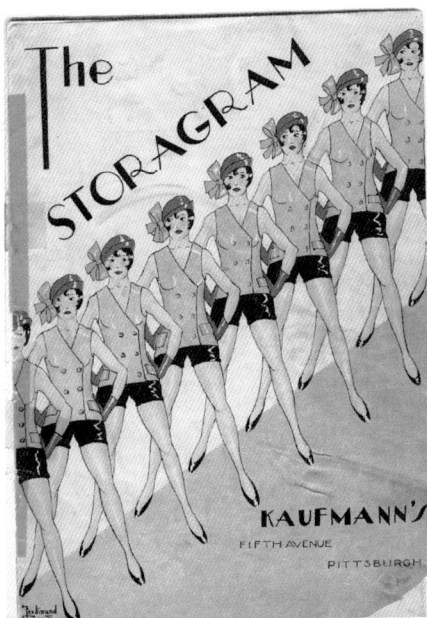

Kaufmann's employees could participate in the Kaufmann Players. The group presented the *Hilarities of 1929*, its fourth production in April, at Pittsburgh's Nixon Theater. The show included singing and dancing, and proceeds supported the store's Beneficial and Protective Association.

a medical exam, membership cost fifty cents per month. Members could receive a weekly cash payment to cover sick time, as well as death benefits for their survivors.

Raising money for the beneficial organization gave employees a chance for fun. In April 1916, they held a "Department Store Carnival and Mardi Gras," the first of its kind. The public was invited to dance, watch a vaudeville show or play euchre. Later, the Kaufmann Players staged a George M. Cohan comic opera, *The Royal Vagabond*, at the Nixon Theater to raise money. A New York actor and his dancer wife trained "store talent," who wore costumes from the original New York presentation. The show was such a success that the players staged *The Firefly* the following year.

The beneficial association had been expanded in 1912 to include an employee hospital and a summer camp. At first, the store hospital was based in a few rooms next to the store kitchen. By the 1920s, it occupied ten rooms on the tenth floor and employed three doctors, three nurses, two dentists and a chiropodist. Employees who became ill at work were required to report to the hospital, where they would either be treated or sent home. If they didn't report back to work after three days, a visiting nurse would be sent to treat them at home.

The hospital also provided annual employee checkups and emergency care to customers. Kaufmann's believed that providing care reduced illness and benefited the store as well as the employees. To promote wellness, medical staff also contributed to the store magazine, the *Storagram*. An article in the 1920s encouraged employees to brush their teeth properly and to floss daily.

The Summer Club managed the Kaufmann camp at Bear Run, 1,700 acres in Fayette County that the store bought from the Shriners. Employees could spend their summer vacations at the camp for as little as seven dollars

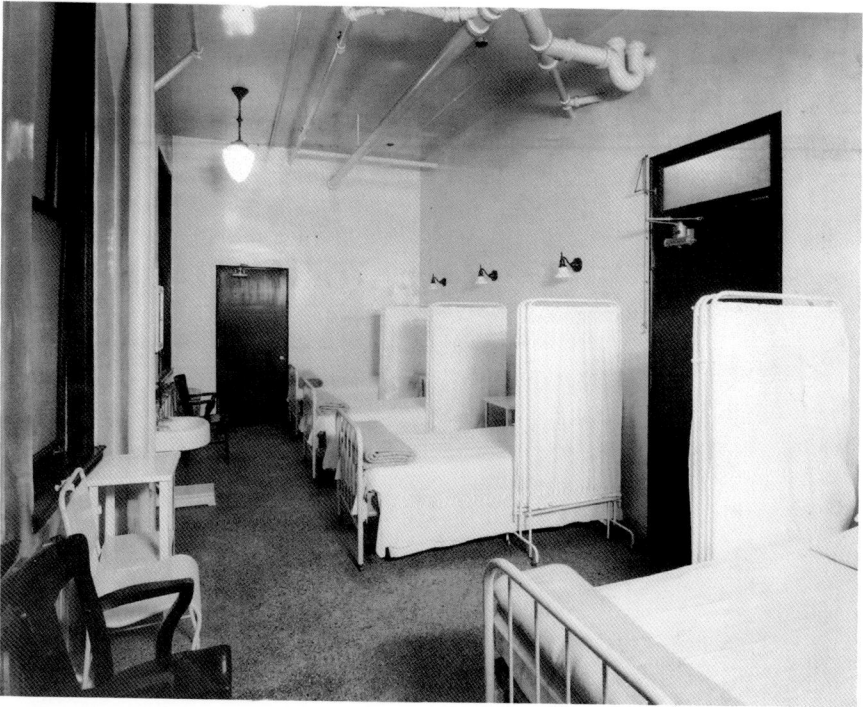

Kaufmann's maintained a hospital in the store for decades. Although it was primarily for employees, customers could be treated in an emergency. An early investment in employee wellness, the hospital was staffed with doctors, dentists, nurses and a chiropodist.

per week. There was a clubhouse with accommodations for seventy girls, family cottages, "back to nature" cottages and a cabin for men. A full-time manager organized costume parties, picnics, hayrides and games; the camp had a swimming pool, tennis courts, golf and hiking trails. There were three hearty meals each day. On weekends, managers, including Liliane and E.J. Kaufmann, visited camp and mingled with employees.

Kaufmann's sponsored numerous recreational opportunities during the year: a bowling team, a chorale club, a baseball team, an orchestra, dances, employee dinners and holiday parties. There was a Women's Club that focused on "the highest ideals in 'Store Life'" and a Men's Club that followed its stag dinner for five hundred with boxing in the store auditorium. After twenty years at the store, employees could join the Stand-By Club, whose members received four weeks of vacation.

In 1920, Kaufmann's launched the *Storagram*, a magazine for employees. It included standard employee milestones—marriages, births, deaths and retirements—as well as articles on store events, cartoons, games and contests. Employees were invited to contribute articles, department news and photos. It changed format and style with the decades, morphing into a standard employee newsletter by the 1970s.

Kaufmann's employees also had access to healthy food without leaving the store. In the earliest days, Kaufmann's had provided Saturday night dinners—a large sandwich, pie and a pail of beer—to those who worked late. Later, a woman would arrive each day with a basket of sandwiches, cakes and pies and set them out on a counter in the employee dining room.

By the 1920s, Kaufmann's had expanded its food service to include a large employee cafeteria on the thirteenth floor that served breakfast and 1,700 to 1,800 lunches daily. A second cafeteria in the North Side warehouse provided breakfast, lunch and Monday dinner for 350 to 400. A Rest and Recreation Room next to the cafeteria included comfortable chairs and lounges where employees could take a quick nap, as well as a large library

Kaufmann's maintained an employee cafeteria in the downtown store and at the North Side warehouse. These women are all appropriately dressed in line with the store's dress code for clerks in the 1920s.

with books and style magazines: *Harper's, Vogue, Ladies' Home Journal, McCall's, Good Housekeeping* and *Woman's Home Companion.* Gertrude Gordon compared the room to a sun parlor in an expensive hotel.

By the late 1940s, Kaufmann's benefits had become comparable to many organizations of the time and recognizable to modern workers: six paid holidays, vacation, a Federal Credit Union that replaced the beneficial association's savings clubs, sick benefits through the association, clubs, the hospital and cafeteria and, one of the most coveted benefits, a 10 percent discount on most items in the store. Kaufmann's also provided tangible career opportunities for women and minorities. The store hired its first female clerk for the glove department in 1914.

From the beginning, many department store employees were women, but the rise of fashion and the need to predict what women would buy opened doors. Women with "fashion instinct" became buyers and department heads. College graduates in fields like home economics were hired as fashionists and in-store restaurant management. Women could flourish in advertising, public relations and event planning. A 1920 article in the *Storagram* entitled "Women in Industry" commented, "Most women, it will be found, are tireless, diplomatic and make some of the most efficient traders and builders.… The women in the department stores of today have more than found their level, they have found the source of their income, their happiness, and their road to bigger business. They are in their own sphere. They can't help but make good if knowledge of merchandise, love of beauty, and honest application lead toward success."

Writing a few years later, Gertrude Gordon noted that many of the women who had been clerks before 1907 were now department heads. She went on to say, "The whole experience only confirmed the general opinion of investigators in working conditions today, that a department store offers the unskilled worker, particularly the girl, more opportunity under better conditions than any other line of employment for which one need not be trained…You have OPPORTUNITY in a department store, no matter how untrained you are, if you only have the will and wish to get ahead."

But that opportunity was constrained by the times. In 1962, a male manager in Kaufmann's publicity department wrote to a recruiter, "What we need, I guess rather urgently now, is a good retail layout person…young man preferred but young woman acceptable." It would be a few more decades before the playing field was really equal.

Minorities were in a similar situation. One black man noted that Kaufmann's was one of the first stores in Pittsburgh to hire black waitstaff

Department stores provided early opportunities for women in business. Smart, ambitious women who were interested in fashion could rise through the ranks from clerk to buyer to department head. Others found opportunities in marketing, public relations, event planning, human resources management and food service management.

in its restaurant. The store's three black porters were longtime employees; in 1921, their tenure ranged from nineteen to twenty-eight years. Kaufmann's also had black elevator operators, as well as craft and warehouse employees. But minorities were not on professional or management staff until late in the twentieth century.

Department stores were challenged, particularly in their early days, by the differences in background between their working-class clerks and middle-class customers. Shoppers complained that clerks were rude, but their behavior was often unintentional—they just didn't understand middle-class life. Many employees had also left school early to work. Stores answered this challenge by developing training programs. The first, in Boston, included lifestyle lessons as well as spelling and math.

Kaufmann's established its own training program in 1921. Developed by Professor Greene from the University of Wisconsin, it initially lasted twenty-six months but was later reduced to twenty-seven weeks. The store supported additional retail training at the University of Pittsburgh.

The *Storagram* was also an important training tool with articles on fashion, "charming home furnishings" and merchandising. Articles reminded sales staff to use proper English and correct terms when describing merchandise: not "cheap" but "inexpensive," not "swell" but "fashionable," not "nifty" but "smart."

Employees also needed guidance on how to dress and behave. Dress codes were strict—for decades, sleeveless dresses were forbidden because they carried the taint of Hollywood. In the 1920s, women at Kaufmann's had to wear very dark-blue or black suits or black skirts and black or dark-blue blouses. Middy blouses were not allowed, nor was jewelry.

By the 1960s, employees could wear simple, tailored clothes in "conservative colors…Black is always perfect." Tweed was allowed, as were carefully coordinated accessories. Later, seasonal employees were reminded

Employees with twenty years of service could join the Stand-By Club. Every year, new members were inducted into the club during a formal banquet. The store's founding brothers, as well as E.J. and Liliane Kauffman, were members of the Stand-By Club.

that no prints or stripes were permitted, nor were earrings or conspicuous makeup. By the end of the decade, the store had relented on both jewelry and makeup, drawing the line at "glittery evening type of jewelry" and "excessive makeup." Women were also told, "Never wear bedroom slippers." Men had dress codes, too: business suits with white or conservative shirts and coordinated ties and hosiery. Coats were to be worn at all times on the selling floor. In the 1960s, sports coats and sports shirts were not allowed.

Employee rules also governed conduct. In the 1920s, Gertrude Gordon reported that clerks were not to talk loudly, call across departments, laugh in the elevator, chew gum or primp at their counters.

Kaufmann's employees seemed content. The ranks of the Stand-By Club were full, and there was little labor strife over the years. When clerks struck Pittsburgh department stores late in the nineteenth century, Kaufmann's told the press that it counted on fair treatment to retain workers. Later, during the yearlong strike of delivery drivers in the 1950s, the press and the public sympathized with the stores, not the strikers. The emphasis on fair treatment continued into the 1970s. Managers were told that proper treatment of employees was the best way to combat union organizing.

The *Storagram* provided one of the best insights into employee culture at Kaufmann's. By the 1970s, it had become less of a magazine and more of a standard employee newsletter, with news from regional stores to announcements of promotions, retirements and key new hires. Content could be clearly tied to management initiatives, especially those that affected the bottom line—loss prevention, safety, health and wellness. Employees received cash awards for recognizing and intercepting lost or stolen credit cards. The store also continued employee activities like picnics and holiday parties.

Longtime loyal employees not only benefited the store but also helped cement relationships with shoppers and regular customers in the restaurant. Many retired employees fondly remembered their days as "Kaufmannites."

Chapter 9

KAUFMANN'S IN THE COMMUNITY

From the earliest days, the Kaufmann brothers—and, by extension, the store they founded—supported the Pittsburgh community. The ill-fated clothing drop of 1883 may have caused a riot, but the store's intentions were good. That the event wasn't just a store promotion was proven by the clothing distributions through social service agencies that followed it.

Kaufmann's community support was varied. The Kaufmann brothers believed that their store could provide entertainment and educational events and staged free concerts in the store and in local parks. They brought educational displays to the city and devoted window space to new technologies, advances in human progress and local organizations. They distributed the Sunday School Greetings picture books for decades at Christmas and provided free holiday entertainment in their windows. Receipts from store sales were donated to social service agencies.

The founding Kaufmann brothers and their descendants also used their personal fortunes to support and promote charitable organizations and personal causes from community services for recent immigrants to urban revitalization of a modern Pittsburgh. Many of the free entertainments were for the customers and were designed to get them into the store or to keep them there. Kaufmann's also provided amusements for its own employees.

One of the most interesting early events was a daylong "excursion for working girls" that Kaufmann's sponsored in summer 1887. The girls, who worked in the shops in Pittsburgh and Allegheny, were treated to a trip on a boat, the *Mayflower*, to Blair's Grove for a picnic. Young men were invited, too, but they had to pay their own way. "Messers. Kaufmann very wisely concluded that the young men ought to be able to pay for their own excursions, and gave all the opportunities of enjoyment to the class working hardest and earning the least, the working girl." There was lemonade by the barrel, a photographer to record the fun and, at the picnic grove, swings, a merry-go-round and orchestra for dancing. At the end of the day, the girls presented a resolution of thanks to the store.

During the 1930s, in-store entertainment provided amusement for people whose budgets wouldn't allow them to buy tickets for concerts or the theater. Community entertainment continued during the war to raise funds for war bond drives and the Red Cross.

Kaufmann's support for community entertainment culminated in E.J. Kaufmann's interest in the Civic Light Opera. In 1946, Kaufmann's Diamond Jubilee, E.J. underwrote the first performance, which was free for

The Flood of 1936 ravaged the Pittsburgh area. Kaufmann's lost $80,000 worth of merchandise when its North Side warehouse flooded. The downtown store collected food for flood relief.

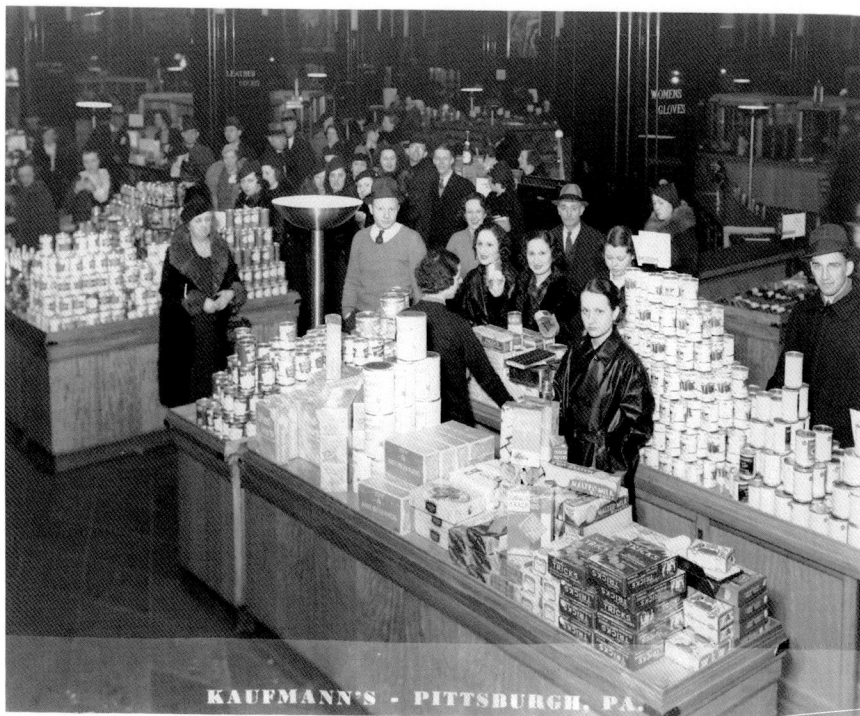

During the 1936 St. Patrick's Day Flood, the largest in Pittsburgh's history, water reached the second floor of Kaufmann's North Side warehouse. In spite of its own losses, the store collected food and supplies for flood victims.

the public. He later donated $1 million toward construction of the Civic Arena where the CLO performed in its early days.

Kaufmann's also donated merchandise and money to a variety of community causes. In 1892, the year of the infamous Homestead Steel Strike, store department managers were asked to select supplies that striking families would most need for donation to the Homestead Fund. Later, when the goods were inventoried, the organizers realized that they didn't have shoes to give. Kaufmann's responded with an additional donation of winter footwear for men, women and children. The store also provided Christmas books and candy for the children so that they "need have no fears that dear old Santa Claus will overlook them."

In June 1896, when the store held a weeklong sale to mark its twenty-fifth anniversary, proceeds from the sale donated to institutions for the needy. Advertisements listed several dozen organizations that would benefit including orphanages and social service agencies. In August 1898,

Kaufmann's donated a percentage of its one-day receipts to the Red Cross for relief of soldiers fighting in the Spanish-American War.

Kaufmann's didn't confine its community gifts to clothing or cash. In March 1911, the store announced that it was distributing 100,000 catalpa trees to students in the Pittsburgh Public Schools. School superintendents outside the city were encouraged to write to the store and ask for trees for their schools. The young trees, eighteen to thirty inches high, would be sent directly to the schools and then given to the children, who were encouraged to plant them at home.

The tree planting, as an attempt to beautify Pittsburgh, would be celebrated on Arbor Day with a practical activity. In the past, children had listened to lectures on conservation. On April 8, the day after Arbor Day, the local press announced, "The 'Big Store's Big Innovation a Big Success."

Catalpas were chosen because they grew quickly, resisted disease and provided shade. They were ornamental when blooming, and their roots would not invade city sewers. But as the trees matured, the children of Pittsburgh discovered that the long seed pods of the "Toby tree" were great fun. Today, the trees are still common in the city.

When Henry Kaufmann sold his store shares to E.J. in the family consolidation, he was able to focus on philanthropy. One of his personal causes was a settlement house in Pittsburgh's Hill district. Established in 1895 by the Council of Jewish Women of Pittsburgh, it was one of the first in the United States. In the beginning, it operated out of a single room, but the settlement later expanded to include public baths and a large public health nursing service. In 1909, Henry and his wife provided funding for a new building and an endowment in their daughter Irene's memory, and the institution was named the Irene Kaufmann Settlement, commonly known as IKS.

IKS focused on strengthening community and family life and providing recreation and education to the community. At the time, the Hill District neighborhood was home to many recent Jewish immigrants from central and eastern Europe; in the 1930s, twenty-one nationalities were represented in the neighborhood.

The settlement provided free baths and laundry facilities, a summer play school, a reading room and recreation rooms. It offered English lessons, art classes and music lessons. In 1926, 25,866 people were enrolled in 1,454 separate classes. There was a theater group and social dances. But IKS wasn't just about recreation. Its staff investigated women's work in stogie factories; studied typhoid fever, slum clearance and low-cost housing; and provided

USE THE GYMNASIUM

Join Today!

IRENE KAUFMANN SETTLEMENT
1835 Center Avenue
Pittsburgh, Pa.

USE THE RECREATION ROOMS

Become a Member Today!

IRENE KAUFMANN SETTLEMENT
1835 Center Avenue
Pittsburgh, Pa.

Left: Henry Kaufmann donated funds as a memorial to his only child, daughter Irene, that allowed a settlement house in the Hill District to expand its activities. The Irene Kaufmann Settlement focused on strengthening the community and providing opportunities for recreation and education. At the time, many of the residents of the neighborhood were recent Jewish immigrants.

Right: In 1926, 25,866 people were enrolled in 1,454 separate classes at the Irene Kaufmann Settlement House. Families in the neighborhood represented twenty-one nationalities, many from eastern Europe.

support during the influenza epidemic. It provided gardens for children and sponsored Better Baby Conferences. One of its most popular activities was a "Milk Well" that sold milk at cost to children in the spring and summer, when families without refrigeration couldn't provide fresh milk.

After his initial support, Henry Kaufmann gave the Irene Kaufmann Settlement additional gifts in 1920 and 1927 that allowed it to expand and again in 1929 and 1939 to strengthen the endowment. In 1940, he celebrated his eightieth birthday with a party at the settlement house and a gift of $25,000. Kaufmann family members were also active as officers and board members of the organization.

In 1957, IKS was renamed the Anna B. Held Community Center and was active until 1962, when many of the buildings were demolished. The Irene Kaufmann Auditorium remained and was restored and reopened to the public in 2011 as the Elsie H. Hillman Theater.

The Emma Farm Association, established by Isaac and Morris Kaufmann in memory of Isaac's wife, Emma, operated under the auspices of the Irene Kaufmann Settlement. The goal of the association was to provide summer vacations in the country for mothers and children from the city. The first farm, operated in Harmony, Pennsylvania, hosted about one thousand guests per summer on what had been a farm school and summer camp for boys.

In 1919, the association bought fifty-two acres in Harmarville for a larger fresh-air farm. There was a dormitory for visitors, dining halls for the children and for staff, a large playroom inside for rainy days, a baseball field and a playground. One of the most popular features was a large outdoor "swimming tank" where girls and boys had separate swimming sessions. Cows, chickens and a truck farm provided fresh food and opportunities for the children to try farm work.

Mothers and children came to the farm in seven groups during the summer. Those in need of country vacations were referred by social service agencies, including the Girls' Welfare Committee, Public Health Nursing Association, Mothers' Assistance Fund, Juvenile Court, Montefiore Hospital Dispensary, Council of Jewish Women and fifteen Pittsburgh public schools. Isaac Kaufmann inspected the farm every Sunday morning during the season and was a popular visitor.

While E.J. Kaufmann was involved in a wide range of philanthropy—he was active in both the Irene Kaufmann Settlement and Emma Farm Association, at Montefiore Hospital and Pittsburgh Jewish organizations—he is often remembered for his interest in the Pittsburgh Renaissance.

One of six incorporators of the Allegheny Conference on Community Development, E.J. developed and presented a plan for a modern, clean, green city to Pittsburghers as part of Kaufmann's seventy-fifth anniversary. Personally charming, he was able to work with the city's Democratic mayor, David Lawrence, and former Republican governor Richard King Mellon. E.J. Kaufmann also commissioned Stefan Lorant to document the renaissance in a large, popular coffee table book.

Kaufmann's community activities continued with the Peaks of Progress in the 1930s, 1940s and 1950s; with decades of support for the local Scholastic Art Awards; and with benefits for local cultural institutions. In 1963, Edgar J. Kaufmann Jr. donated the family's summer home, Fallingwater, to the

Kaufmann's participated in community parades. This float advertises the annual store anniversary celebrated every June.

Western Pennsylvania Conservancy, which opened the Frank Lloyd Wright masterpiece to the public the following year. By the 1980s, Kaufmann's was sponsoring or co-sponsoring Pittsburgh's Great Race, Celebrate the Season parade, Symphony Ball, fundraising activities for the Civic Light Opera, the WQED auction, the Carnegie Museum of Art Annual Benefit and benefit fashion shows.

Chapter 10

MOVING TO SUBURBIA

*D*uring his lifetime, E.J. Kaufmann lobbied for branch stores in the suburbs. Competitor Joseph Horne's had made the move in 1945 to suburban Mt. Lebanon. Apparently, he wasn't able to convince others on the management team. But E.J. was committed not only to the downtown store but also to urban renewal. And yet, as one historian noted, "urban renewal was a disaster for the downtown economy and the local department store."

In Pittsburgh, urban renewal led to destruction of downtown neighborhoods whose residents shopped in the city. Federal funding provided money to construct highways out of the city, and tax policies made new construction more cost effective than restoration of existing real estate. Popular culture celebrated suburbia. Kaufmann's "House on the Roof" may have been downtown, but the model homes just like it were all in the suburbs.

Most department stores expanded into suburbia. Kaufmann's joined them in March 1961, opening a 200,500-square-foot free-standing store in Monroeville, Pennsylvania. The store reflected the downtown flagship with air conditioning, escalators, charge accounts and phone shopping. There was a Tic Toc Restaurant, an Adoria Beauty Salon and a "thrifty Downstairs Store." And there was parking for 1,500 cars.

The Monroeville store was followed in summer 1965 with a second suburban store in Mt. Lebanon. "Curtain Going Up On a Marvelous New Production," declared the advertising. "It's a Showplace…all the sparkle, shimmer, and shine of a bright new musical." Mt. Lebanon shoppers who had once traveled downtown could now shop around the corner. The new

Kaufmann's Monroeville store opened in March 1961 with parking for 1,500 cars, air conditioning, escalators and a Tic Toc Restaurant. The free-standing store was later closed, and Kaufmann's moved to the Monroeville Mall.

The groundbreaking for the Monroeville store was a major community event complete with ribbon cutting and music from a high school band.

store also had a Tic Toc Restaurant and an Adoria Beauty Salon, as well as parking for nine hundred cars in a three-level covered garage.

The next spring, Kaufmann's McKnight opened, "the complete department store in the North Hills." It, too, had free parking, a Tic Toc Restaurant, a beauty salon and a basement bargain store. Advertisements showed a map so shoppers north of the city could find the newest suburban Kaufmann's.

But moving to the suburbs didn't necessarily help department stores compete in the retail arena. Available financing favored shopping malls that were anchored by chain stores like Penney's and Sears. Chain stores and discounters like Kmart and Walmart dominated retail and catered to growing consumerism. They taught shoppers to expect low prices. Department stores struggled to compete.

Like other department stores, Kaufmann's embraced the mall, opening in Ohio's Fort Steuben Mall in 1974. Explaining a similar store in the Beaver Valley Mall, a store executive said, "This store represents a change in Kaufmann's marketing philosophy.... During our first expansion period

In the spring of 1966, Kaufmann's opened "the complete department store in the North Hills on McKnight Road." Like other suburban stores, McKnight had free parking, a Tic Toc Restaurant, a beauty salon and a basement bargain store.

While Kaufmann's first suburban stores were free-standing buildings in prime shopping areas, the store opened its first mall store in 1974. Kaufmann's mall stores were often mall anchors. As a store executive explained, "Shopping malls are consistent with a new consumer lifestyle." This artist's rendering illustrates the Kaufmann's mall location in Erie, Pennsylvania.

in the 1950s free standing stores met the needs of our customers. However, the shopping malls are consistent with a new consumer lifestyle." Soon there were mall stores in Millcreek, Erie; Century III; South Hills Village; and Beaver Valley.

As a division of the May Company, Kaufmann's absorbed other department stores, including Strouss (1986), based in Youngstown, Ohio; Sibley's (1991), based in Rochester, New York, which had merged with Hengerer's (1981) of Buffalo, New York; May Company Ohio (1992), based in Cleveland, Ohio, which had merged with O'Neil's (1989) in Akron, Ohio; and, in 1995, the remnants of McCurdy's stores of Rochester and Hess's of Allentown, Pennsylvania. Many of these stores were in shopping malls.

The free-standing stores were closed, and in 1986, a developer bought three of them—Mt. Lebanon, Rochester in Beaver County and McKnight. The former McKnight store was moved to anchor the new Ross Park Mall.

In spite of the emphasis on suburbia, there was still plenty of action downtown. In the 1960s, Kaufmann's college activities were centered on the flagship store with its large college shop. It sold miniskirts, Capezio shoes and fashions by "mod" designers like Mary Quant. The store recruited a

"College Board," eighteen students from local colleges and the Ivy League, who were photographed in a "suspender shift" inspired by Courreges and worn with matching sweater and tights. The outfit was for sale in the store.

The College Board members modeled "Campus Fashions '65" at a Friday the Thirteenth College Show on August 13 at 7:30 p.m. in the Penn Sheraton Hotel Ballroom. The show was free, with a ticket from the College Shop or the Clay Poole Shop—boys were invited, too.

The Peaks of Progress and June anniversary events continued throughout the 1950s and early 1960s, drawing national attention to Kaufmann's. The topics reflected national issues: atomic energy, space exploration, the European Common Market, the digital computer and the Peace Corps. In the final year of the event, 1964–65, the leading "Peak" was the Civil Rights Act of 1964. A Bell Telephone presentation discussed "Reaching for the Moon." Anniversary sales continued during the next decades, but the end of "Peaks of Progress" signaled the end of the anniversary as a major store event.

In 1970, the store also developed a new initiative to appeal to working women who didn't have the leisure to shop: Triangle Corner Limited—Kaufmann's Program for Women in Business. It sponsored college classes, special events, fashion shows and networking during lunch hours and at the end of the workday. Triangle Corner recognized the emerging interests of working women in management training, financial planning and business fashion and responded accordingly for two decades.

Kaufmann's renovated the first floor of the downtown store in 1983 to increase selling space and upgrade the décor. The pillars were covered with mirrored glass, incandescent lighting replaced fluorescent fixtures and rose, mauve and plum became the new colors.

People also came to Kaufmann's to eat. By the 1990s, the store included thirteen food stops—restaurants, specialty food stations and bakeries. There were three dining rooms on the eleventh floor: the white tablecloth Forbes Room, the less formal Edgar's and the family-oriented Michael's. Shoppers could buy hot dogs, sandwiches, pizza or salads at four cafés. For ice cream—made on the premises—there was Temptations on the ninth floor, a 1950s-style ice cream parlor. Food carts offered bagels, muffins and cookies. For many people, the iconic Tic Toc on the first floor was still the place to meet for a burger or ice cream pie. And for employees, there was the cafeteria on the thirteenth floor.

Cooks in the Kaufmann's kitchens created almost everything from scratch using a thick manual of recipes dating back a century. In the

Arcade Bakery, more than two hundred items were baked daily, including twenty different kinds of jumbo muffins from twenty different recipes. Kaufmann's served almost six thousand meals daily prepared by a staff of more than 260. Some of the cooks had been working at the store for more than thirty years. At a time when retail was struggling, the store food operations actually made a profit.

By 1990, the *Wall Street Journal* was noting that the May Company was still thriving as other department store companies struggled. Its CEO had risen through the ranks at Kaufmann's, which may have helped the store retain its local identity as long as it did.

But there were signs of trouble on the horizon. The Vendôme was shuttered because few Pittsburgh women were willing to pay full price for designer clothing. In 1993–94, the Boardman Robinson murals, which had been in storage for decades, were sold to the Colorado Fine Arts Center. E.J. Kaufmann's store office designed by Frank Lloyd Wright had already been dismantled and sold to the Victoria and Albert Museum. In March 1999, Kaufmann's held its final warehouse sale before its North Side warehouse was sold.

In May 2002, in a May consolidation designed to save $60 million, Kaufmann's headquarters was moved from Pittsburgh to Boston and its management combined with Filene's. Buyers, managers and administrative staff would be moving; 850 people were laid off in the spring and an additional 347 in July when the store's credit center was closed.

Even with consolidation, May Company could not compete with Walmart and the other big-box stores. In 2005, the mega-merger between Federated Department Stores and the May Company was, to some, the end of the local department store. Many iconic stores, including Filene's and Marshall Field's, were rebranded as Macy's.

And so was Kaufmann's. On September 9, 2006, Federated Department Stores converted the regional store into Macy's. The original brass plaques with the Kaufmann's name were still on the store building, and the clock remained on the corner. Macy's kept the original Tic Toc Restaurant and the Arcade Bakery and sponsored the traditional holiday parade. But Kaufmann's as a store was then just a memory.

Chapter 11

MEMORIES OF KAUFMANN'S

*F*rom the very beginning, Kaufmann's was a special store, and customers and employees developed fond memories of their days there. Over the years, these memories appeared in the local press and in the store magazine, the *Storagram*. Here are some of those memories.

ISAAC KAUFMANN, 1912

From Pittsburgh Post, *"Looking Back Forty-Four Years," June 1, 1912.*

Forty-four years ago (I wonder how many of us can look back that far and remember our little store and its few counters of goods out there on the South Side) my brother and I founded this firm.

Between us we had $1,500 in cash, but we were millionaires in hope and confidence—filled with boyish faith Faith in ourselves and in the young city which had begun to stir with vast ambitions—pitting youth and energy against the coming years.

And we had one thing else, an asset that grew as we went—this piece of advice from the good father who sacrificed his own happiness to send his sons into a strange land which would give us opportunities that our birthplace could not promise:

Sell to others as you would buy for yourself.
  Good merchants make small profits and many sales.
  Deal fairly—be patient and in time your dishonest competitors will
crowd your store with customers.

It is a long time since these words were spoken. Meanwhile, the world has improved almost everything it holds, but I don't believe that a better piece of wisdom has ever been offered to a young man starting out on his career—the walls of this great store of ours rest upon that foundation…

44 years ago—how I recall that stern and poverty-stricken period—we couldn't have picked out a worse stretch of years.

The average family could afford but the barest necessities of life. A dollar was a big piece of silver—sufficient to feed and clothe and house a man and a wife and children.

We were living in a frontier period. The continent was still in the making.

A few miles away were entire villages of whose inhabitants had never been on a railroad or seen the sea. A horse car was a novelty. Travel by power was confined to queer little, rickety, steam railroads.

Gas light was a marvel and kerosene (actually sold as patent medicine, to cure the most ridiculous range of ills) was being experimented with for household illumination…. There was not an electric motor on earth, nor a typewriter nor a talking machine.

Bell hadn't built a telephone, and we used to tap our heads when we heard anyone talk about flying machines.

SEVERAL LONGTIME EMPLOYEES, 1917–18

From Storagram, *"In Anniversary Days Gone By," June 1941.*

Kaufmann's employees remembered the store's 46th anniversary during World War I.

Max Odenheimer, Manager of the Alterations Department…remembers particularly that to save electricity there were no lights on and no elevator service before 10 A.M. (Of course, there were no escalators at all in the store back then.) About sugar, he says, "You could not buy sugar in grocery stores, but the firm bought sugar and resold it to their employees. One night a week as we went out we stood in line to buy one pound of sugar—it cost about 21c."

Marie Maloney, Personnel Department. "The biggest problem the store had was in getting help—we employed high school students to work after school, women to work short hours. If any employee could bring in another person to work who would stay a minimum of two months, the employee was awarded $5.00. She told us, too, about 'Fuel-less Mondays'—on which day the store was closed to save fuel. But some of the non-selling people came to work a half day—wearing sweaters and coats to keep warm. Two nights a week about 300 women worked for the Red Cross on the 11th floor, making surgical dressings under the direction of Mrs. E.J. Kaufmann. Training was very limited. 'A new salesperson was hurridly [*sic*] given some instructions about making out saleschecks and a few rules about the store and then rushed to the department to be put on the job.'"

Simon Adelsheim, Second Floor Superintendent. "We cut our C.O.D.'s altogether. No returns were allowed unless the customer brought the merchandise back in person within 3 days after purchase. We were very strict then. The government did not try to control prices then, but the firm did all they could to protect the public."

LONGTIME SALES CLERK, 1921

From Storagram, *"Sales and Tales that Are Told Reminiscences of an Old Timer," July–August, 1921.*

Peter Kline as told to I. Hohenstein.

Peter Kline who worked for the Big Store in the Pup Kilt Suit Department about forty years ago, said to me one day, "Ike, if this store ever forms a strategy board, I will certainly recommend you for its president, as that was a very clever stunt you just pulled and it certainly deserves recognition." At that time, I didn't exactly know what he meant by strategy (as I was only a boy then) but I supposed he had reference to a sale we made that day under very peculiar circumstances.

At the period…we were located on the other side of Smithfield at the corner of Diamond Alley. We occupied the two storerooms at the corner and while we had two entrances, the interior of the store was all one. Between the two stores on the outside we had from 50 to 60 dummies and other means of displaying our wares.

One day, in walked a man who wanted to look at an overcoat. At that time we carried our men's overcoats on the second floor (we had no basement store then) and the only means we had of getting to it was to walk up. About three-fourths of an hour after, I happened to be talking to Aaron Lehman when I noticed this customer coming down stairs and a salesman trailing behind with an overcoat in his hands. I heard the customer say, "Well, if you don't want to sell it for $15.00, you can keep it." The salesman after another futile effort to sell him the overcoat at $18.00 (which was $3.00 above the cost) very mournfully let him walk out.

There was a little gloom in the store for a few moments after he had gone because missing a sale in those days was a sad event.

However time heals all wounds and after a few minutes of razzing, we forgot about it. About fifteen minutes later, I happened to see this same customer come in the other entrance and of course, naturally supposed he had come back for the overcoat. I approached him expecting him to say, "Well, I guess I'll take that coat," but to my astonishment, he simply asked to look at an overcoat. It dawned on me in a flash that he thought he was in another store and right here is where Pete Kline accused me of being a strategist. I said, "Just a minute," and then quickly went over to Pete and said, "Keep him interested while I run upstairs." I ran upstairs and hastily explained the circumstances...and suggested that some salesman should wait on him other than the man who had tried to sell him before...A fresh salesman greeted him, and in a few minutes sold him the same coat which he had refused to buy before for $18.00 for $22.50. Never dreaming that it was the same coat or the same store, he walked away...

P.S.—This was long before the Store adopted the one price policy.

MISS NETTIE MCKENZIE, DIRECTOR OF EMPLOYEE WELFARE, 1925

From Nettie McKenzie, "In Days Gone By and Now," Storagram, 1925.

The editor has asked me to tell the readers of the STORAGRAM something about the store as it was when I first came.

One day a friend came to where I was employed and said, "I am working at Kaufmann's," and asked me to come. Mr. Henry Kaufmann employed me that day for the Millinery Department, and I commenced work the following morning.

I was not superstitious, as I was hired on Friday and started work on Saturday. At that time there was the original building of five stories and basement; two entrances, one on Fifth Avenue and the other on Smithfield, and one small elevator.

That year the first addition was made on Fifth Avenue, almost to Cherry Way on the Methodist church property. Stairways in the center of the building up to the fifth floor, and the new and larger elevators were put in. The next addition, I believe, was Mechanical Hall on Diamond Street, and from time to time more buildings were added until the store covered the entire block…

The Millinery Department was on the Fifth Avenue side, four small cases, two at each end, were for trimmed hats, and six tables for untrimmed ones in the center. To one side were cases for ribbons, feathers and flowers. These third floor departments had not been in existence very long. Women did not buy ready-made gowns. Coats and furs were the principal stocks then.

In the Millinery Department all hats were trimmed and made in our work rooms, except the "pattern hats." I remember the first ready-trimmed hats brought into the department. I was given charge of them and "good sellers" were reordered all season. Styles did not change overnight then as they do today.

We had calls in the Millinery Department. I was fourth, and no matter whether I approached a customer first or not, I could not wait on her unless the other three were busy.

With every addition made in the store the Millinery and Ladies' Suit Departments were enlarged, until today we have one of the best departments for women's apparel in the city, and of course, I always think Kaufmann's Millinery Department is just about right.

On the completion of the first addition these new departments were added on the first floor: silks, dress goods, linens, wash goods, neckwear, laces, embroideries, ribbons and handkerchiefs and later jewelry, books, hosiery and leather goods.

The girls were permitted to come to the store later than the men and leave a few minutes earlier. You registered your time at the cashier's desk at Smithfield Street door. The girl's wraps were checked on the fourth floor, and Mr. Archie Greiner, now our head window dresser, was then in charge of the check room. In the evenings our wraps were placed on the trunks in that department. Later on we had wooden lockers on the sixth floor, and we called our numbers to the timekeeper as we passed. This system was in use for years. Many employees will remember it.

In those days all stores were open until 6 P.M. and the majority until 10:00 P.M. on Saturdays. During the Christmas holiday season all stores were open every evening in 9 P.M. at least two weeks before Christmas. These hours continued until 1903.

In 1913 the remodeling took place and we have the building as it is today. The time office was removed to the eighth floor, and steel lockers on every floor with individual compartments for hats have replaced the old system entirely.

In the early days members of the firm and buyers did the hiring. Then later the general superintendent took over some of the employing. A small record card of the employees was kept in the office. Application blanks were not used.

The office, which was located on the fourth floor, was very small, with I believe, three employees. It included the paymaster's office, and on pay day employees went there for their pay.

The contrast today is striking, with our large general, auditing, credit, paymaster, employment and other offices.

About April, 1913, the employment bureau was added, under the direction of the general superintendent. We then had four people in the office, the employment manager, two clerks and a messenger. It was then that we introduced the application blank. References were requested and other employment records installed. I remember when the employment office sent around the new form of application blanks, requesting all employees to fill out same. Many did not want to fill them out when they had been employed here for so long. Old employees were not asked to give references, but it was necessary to have their correct name and address and other general information.

Later, in 1914, when Mr. Wm. T. Gore, our former superintendent came, the original system was improved upon, and more records were necessary in the Employment Department. We then had two people who did the hiring, and four clerical workers. Then things went along until we now have our present personnel bureaus with its staff of employment supervisors and record office.

I forgot to mention our cash system. We used baskets run by pulleys and overhead wrapping desks with cashiers and wrappers in them. Mrs. Tinnemeyer, who is now our head cashier, was one of the cashiers. We also had some cashiers' desks scattered through departments.

The marking and receiving room was on the fifth floor and on dull days we were sometimes sent up to mark and ticket goods. Mr. Thomas Flynn, the present manager, was a boy in the department at that time.

After the first addition a space was given to employees for a dining room. A long room with a counter at one end. A woman from the outside came in every day at 11 o'clock with a large basket containing sandwiches, cakes, pies and so forth. A little later on the employees restaurant was taken over by the manager of the public dining room, then on the eighth floor. Improvements were added from time to time until we now have our present employees dining room on the eighth floor.

There are so many things today in "The Big Store" for the employees that were utterly unknown in former years—the Beneficial Association, hospital, doctor, nurse, dentist, nurse to visit employees in their homes, library, magazines, orchestra, woman's club, culture classes, vacation savings club and personnel division.

GERTRUDE GORDON, PITTSBURGH JOURNALIST AND FORMER KAUFMANN'S EMPLOYEE, 1925

From Storagram, *"Gertrude Gordon Pays 'The Big Store' a Visit," January 1925.*

Various assignments, listed under the head of personal experience, fall to the lot of the feature writer, so, when one day, recently, the city editor of the *Press* said, "Go to Kaufmann's tomorrow and work in the store all day, then write up what happens," the order, although a little surprising, was not startling.

So, after going through all of the procedures required of new employees, the next morning saw me at the glove department, where with only the employees' relief hours, I stood all day.

Of course, it was interesting, meeting the customers and working with the girls, but, as is so happened, it was not a new thing to me.

For this was the thirteenth time I had worked at Kaufmann's. Every other time was in the capacity of real employee, in the years before newspaper work claimed me, and I was absorbed in my own reactions to coming back; just for the experience, not for necessity.

The clock of time ticked back 17 years when I reported to duty that day, for it had been that long since I was employed in the Big Store. But it ticked back farther and farther, until it stopped at my fifteenth birthday, for that marked my first day's work.

After several weary days of applying, with other girls of like age, for the coveted position, on this particular day it was given me. The work was only extra, that is it lasted just three days. It was several years before I returned, and then it was in the capacity of demonstrator in the grocery department.

Several demonstrations fell to my lot during the ensuing years, at intervals with other work, outside the store, also positions as a regular employee of the store until in 1907, I left, finally, to take a position at the *Pittsburgh Post* in the circulation department. In June 1908, I began with the *Press* as feature writer and have been there ever since.

So it was not actually a new thing to seek and get a job. But the unusual thing about it was the general atmosphere surrounding such job getting today, as contrasted to years ago.

Long time ago, when you were given work in a department store, you were given a locker key, a slip of paper telling your floorwalker who you were, and that was all. Your instructions as to sales-slips, privileges, duties and rules came from your fellow-workers. Sometimes the floorwalker had time to tell you, particularly if you were a little slow at assimilating the knowledge, but ordinarily, you learned just as you could.

The rest room for the women employees those days was small, uncomfortable, with no easy chairs. In fact the only chairs were brought up from the shoe department. No magazines lay around, no carpet was on the floor…

There was no summer camp…

The hours in the store were what those in charge choose to make them. And most days, department store work meant…working until 10 P.M. every day at holiday season. Also every Saturday the store closed at 10 P.M.

Today the contrast is like realizing a Utopian dream.

This contrast can be illustrated best by my own experiences…

First came the making out of the application blank and, when that is done there is very much about the prospective employee which the store officials do not know and check…

Then I was conducted to the training room. This was an absolutely new idea to me.

About 25 of us were in the in the room together in chairs fitted with wide arms for comfort in writing. Each of us had a salesbook and an index.

Facing us was a blackboard with, on it, similes of the store sales-checks we were to make out.

But before this instruction came, a vivid, attractive young blond girl who gave us a remarkably comprehensive talk on the store itself. First, she told the employees their privileges. This included the Summer Camp, the care taken of them when ill, the special prices allowed them by the store, the benefits of the Mutual Beneficial Association. She talked on store Loyalty, told why Kaufmann's is the best store, why its prices are as low or lower than elsewhere, quality considered, its goods of the highest quality, its customers the best satisfied.

She suggested rules of conduct, particularly for the girls. She gently advised no loud talking, no talking with, when customers stood waiting, no primping at the counters, no laughing or chattering in the elevators, no calling across a department, no wearing of jewelry or sleeveless dresses, or use of too much rouge or powder.

Things I learned are these: If an employee is ill, he is required to report to the hospital. If ill enough to go home, he is sent there. If off work for several days, a visiting nurse goes to the house, and here the social services department gets to work. Sometimes the nurse finds bad home surroundings for a girl or boy, or finds extreme poverty. Tactfully, knowledge of this is given to some person who can help better conditions. Of course, all this information was not part of the instruction given that day, but it happens that I know of the excellent social service work done in the store through this visiting nurse.

One requirement is made of any employee ill more than a couple of days—that is that he keeps in touch with the hospital. If he is away more than three weeks, his position is held for him, after that time, no surety is given, but, if possible he is taken care of until he returns.

After an employee has been with the store two months, he can draw a benefit of $8 a week through the beneficial association. A death benefit also goes with membership in this organization…

Then we were all taken on a tour of the hospital, the rest rooms, and the cafeteria.

The hospital had private rooms in addition to the dormitory, a nurse is in constant attendance, and a physician and dentist at certain hours.

Everything is the way of medicine is there and competent advice is given to those who are ill.

Another new idea in service to the employees—an attorney is in an office in the store on certain days and his advice is free to those who desire it.

On the little tour of inspection we found the rest room so pretty it might be a sun parlor in an expensive hotel. Soft lights, wide windows, easy chairs make it a place of rest and relaxation.

A branch of the Carnegie Library is there and employees of the store may take out books just like they could at the Library.

The wash-rooms for the employees are appointed every bit as well as those for customers—also a new idea.

The young blond finished with us, by explaining that chewing gum or eating candy during working-hours was forbidden. She urged the uniform dressing in dark colors...

Then came an efficient little brunet who explained the sales-slips. We all had to make out the various kinds paid for and taken, change and taken, paid for and sent, and charged and sent. Again, questions were encouraged. Then we were shown how to work the cash registers.

We were advised, in case of difficulty, always to report it immediately to the floorwalker, and not to depend on another salesperson's advice.

Little bits of good advice were given. For instance, "If you are at a cash register and forget to put the money in until after the drawer is shut—which often happens," said our instructor, "don't hold the money in your hand until the next sale. Tell the floor manager and he will open the register for you. For, although perfectly honest, yet someone might see you keep that money and it wouldn't look right."

How to fend off a customer's complaints and satisfy them was told. How to ease away a charge customer's impatience while the credit department was checking his or her account was suggested.

Care of the store's goods was urged.

Surely, every person went away from that room, with a good, fundamental knowledge of how to sell.

It was a far cry from that day in the years agone, when a slip of paper and command to go to a certain department constituted the whole instruction given.

At noon, I went to the employee cafeteria and the joy of it! The airy-sunny room, the appetizing display of food, the courteous service, the general air of busy restfulness, such a paradox can be imagined was a revelation.

Speaking of the summer camp at Bear Run, having visited it, and having visited also its predecessor, the Emma Farm near Harmarville, I knew that when its charms were being explained, they all had foundation in fact.

One scarcely could imagine a more ideal place for a vacation than the camp. Roomy dormitories and cottages, a swimming-pool, grounds for tennis and even golf, acres and acres of private ground to roam over, splendid food, and three-times-a-day plentiful meals make it a close approach to Eden.

John Eberle, Longtime Employee, 1931

From John Eberle, "My First Fifty Years in the Store," Storagram, 1931.

Fifty years ago an energetic youngster named John Eberle approached Isaac Kaufmann, one of the four Kaufmann brothers who founded the store, and asked, "Mr. Kaufmann, can you give me a job?"

Mr. Kaufmann looked at the youngster, asked him several questions and then said, "I need an extra hand in the Supply Room. Think you can handle the job?"

"Yes, sir!" young John quickly replied. "Then be here at 8 o'clock tomorrow morning, and if you are a good boy, you'll have a steady job with us." Mr. Kaufmann told him.

Well, John must have been a good boy because this year Mr. Eberle celebrated his fiftieth year as an active Kaufmann employee. In appreciation of his faithful and outstanding service, Kaufmann's presented him with a $1,000 check at the Stand-By club Dinner in May.

Needless to say, Mr. Eberle has seen many, many changes and improvements since he started in the store 50 years ago. In an interview, he recalled many pertinent and interesting facts which could easily fill a volume. However, due to lack of space, we will touch only the highlights of his "First Fifty Years in the Store."

"When I first started," he recalled, "Kaufmann's was at its present site. The store consisted of five stories and a basement and had two entrances, one on Fifth Avenue and one on Smithfield Street. The one elevator we had was quite unlike the streamlined ones today. We ran that one by hand cable."

He continued, "In those days all stores were open from 8 a.m. to 6 p.m. and most of them were open from 8 a.m. to 10 p.m. on Saturdays. During Christmas holidays we were open every evening until 9. When we went home after work we delivered packages to the customers who lived nearby…

"The main business in early years was clothing. Men's and Boy's Clothing took up the entire Second Floor; Basement had House Furnishings; first floor Men's Furnishings and Hats and Shoes; Third Floor Women's and Misses' Coats, Underwear and Millinery. On the Fourth Floor was the Main Office, Trunk Department and a Check Room for employees' wraps. The Marking and Receiving Department was on the Fifth Floor and on dull days we were sent up to mark and ticket goods.

He added, "I remember quite well when the first addition to the present building was made on Fifth Avenue to Cherry Way. The employees and customers said it was sensational when we subsequently added a grand stairway. The Downstairs Store opened in 1915 and became a major division in 1924.

"It is really amazing to stroll through the store these days and see the many improvements made since I first started. To me, the most outstanding improvements were the redesigning and rebuilding of the First Floor in 1930, the installation of 66 escalators and the present new stainless steel elevators. When I look at the store-wide air conditioning now being installed, I think about the earlier days when a fan in the department was a rare luxury, one we never let out of our sight.

"We really worked hard in the early days. There was no such thing as a 15-minute relief period. Nor did we have the present Hospitalization Insurance, a hospital with a staff of doctors, nurses and dentists, the benefit of a Training Department, vacations, and so many, many things the present-day employees are enjoying that were utterly unknown in former years.

"In the early days, members of the firm and buyers did the hiring. Then later the general superintendent took over some of the employing. A small record card of the employees was kept in the main office. Application blanks were not used. The main office, which was located on the Fourth Floor, was very small and had only three employees. It included the paymaster's office, and on pay days employees went there for their pay. The contrast today is very striking, with our large general, auditing, paymaster, employment and other offices.

"In 1913 the Employment Bureau was added, under the direction of the general superintendent. We then had four people in the office, the Employment Manager, two clerks, and a messenger. It was then that prospective employees first began using application blanks. I can remember when the new Employment Office sent around the new form and requested all employees to fill out same. Many did not want to fill them out because they had been employed in the store so long. Old employees were not requested to give references, but it was necessary for them to give their correct name and address."

Mr. Eberle spent most of his 50 years with the Supply Room, but hastened to add that "we had to perform other duties too. If one department was very busy, we dropped what we were doing and rushed to help. I can remember when an extra-duty job required me to blow up balloons for eight solid hours—and by mouth. I must have been a windy fellow in those days," he laughed.

Although he isn't taking all the credit for Mr. Edgar J. Kaufmann's present position as president of Kaufmann's, Mr. Eberle said he "remembers the day when I was in charge of Mr. Kaufmann. His father, Mr. Morris Kaufmann, said he wanted 'Edgar to learn the business from the bottom up.' He placed him under my care in the Supply Room. Every day the father would drop by and say, 'How is Edgar doing?' I answered that he's coming along just fine. I certainly was telling the truth, too, because look at him today!"

In conclusion, Mr. Eberle said, "One thing I can say about Kaufmann's is that the store was never second with anything. Always first. That is why it has also been a pleasure and an honor for me to tell people that I work at Kaufmann's. I enjoyed that pleasure when Mr. Kaufmann treated me with courtesy and kindness when I asked for a job. I liked working at Kaufmann's from the start. I still like working at Kaufmann's—after fifty years."

Early Shoppers, 1942

From Pittsburgh Post-Gazette, *May 28, 1942.*

Annie A. Jones, of Glassport, whose family has shopped at Kaufmann's since the first year of the store's life, reminisces of the day when her mother bought her brothers their first "store coats" at Kaufmann's on Carson street—"blue chinchilla overcoats with capes attached."

John A. Kelly, of Ridge Avenue, remembers the day when he, a lad of eight, was taken by his grandmother to Kaufmann's new store on Smithfield Street, to buy a new suit. "The suit was wonderful enough, but with each suit Kaufmann's was giving a Waterbury watch," he chuckles. "I have owned a good many watches since, but never had one that to me seemed so shiny and bright and that ticked so loud. I'm still shopping at Kaufmann's, not only for myself but also for my grandson."

William Robinson, Longtime Waiter, 1985

From Jerry Vondas, "This Waiter Has Served Shoppers Since 1930," Pittsburgh Press, January 22, 1985.

There were three of us when I came to Kaufmann's Jan. 21, 1930. There were no waitresses. Only waiters. We were all black men...all excellent waiters.... One day my cousin pointed out the Kaufmann waiters to me.

They were all impeccably dressed, very friendly and highly respected. I said to myself, "That's what I want."

...I applied and was told I'd have to wait. There was a long list. But I was persistent and finally got the job. It was a great day for me. Kaufmann's dining room was considered one of the finest in the city. In those days they carried shad and roe on the menu as well as lobster thermidor, shrimp, turtle soup and oysters and clams on the half shell. I had to train as a busboy for months before the headwaiter permitted me to start taking my own orders.

Harry Stewart was our headwaiter. He was considered one of the best. The Kaufmann family brought him from New York City to direct the dining rooms. Stewart was tough. He had us stand for inspection every morning. If your nails weren't properly trimmed or your shoes polished, he'd send you back to the locker room. If you talked back to him, it was an automatic three-day suspension without pay. Stewart had an eagle eye. He would watch you from every corner of the dining room.

I remember during one lunch Stewart handed the menus to his assistant and crossed the room to reprimand a waiter who was chewing gum. He warned the waiter that if he was caught chewing gum again, it would mean his job. But we respected him. Even after he retired I'd often visit him...

When I started at Kaufmann's William McNair was the mayor of Pittsburgh. I've waited on about every mayor since. Who could forget a mayor like the late David L. Lawrence? Even after he became governor he would stop in and have lunch when he was in the city.

...Mr. Wolf was a big man and a big eater. Every day for lunch he would put away a large tureen of soup before ordering. Edgar Kaufmann liked spinach and Oliver Kaufmann wasn't too fussy. I waited on their mother for several years. She was a gracious lady.

...I doubt we'll ever see the day again when department store restaurants will carry the elaborate menus that they did in our day.

FASHION DIRECTOR, 1998

From Georgia Sauer, "Wholesalechanges," Pittsburgh Post-Gazette, *November 10, 1996.*

A Pittsburgh fashion writer interviews Joanne Pagnanelli Kaufmann's Vice President and Merchandising Director about her 25 years at the store beginning in 1971.

"The Downtown store was really like a city within a city. We had our own pharmacy when I started 25 years ago, and a doctor on call and a nurse on duty all the time. There were about 5,500 employees at the four Kaufmann's then; now we have 14,000 at the 47 stores…

"Our bakery baked everything Downtown for the four stores, and then shipped it out to the other stores. We had our own brand of tissue paper then, of soaps, of bath powders, even toilet paper. Millinery was huge on the fourth floor. We even had our own Kaufmann's hat box.

"We sold whole kitchens of cabinets and appliances, dinette sets, paints, special-order wallpaper, hardware; we sold screws and custom-made curtains.

"I'm lucky because I got into retailing when it was very exciting and creative. The customer then expected newness and excitement and creativity. Shopping was then more of an experience. Retailers were expected to make shopping an event. Now with so many working women shopping has become more of a necessity than a social outing. We don't have time to shop; we have so many other priorities. Now selection and pricing is what the customer expects.

"It's a different world out there. There are so many retailers out there, so many discounters that we're always thinking of sales promotion events. That's the world of retailing today.

"Kaufmann's was then retailing royalty. We had corporate offices in Paris and Florence and they would arrange our trips.

"The emphasis used to be one-on-one with the customer, in fashion shows and luncheons we would put on. I used to spend a ton of time planning them. Now my job is merchandizing—buying the right merchandise, presenting it [in ads and visually on the floor and windows], and selling it. It's a major team effort.

"My job is very, very different that it would have been 25 years ago. We used to have about 80 major fashion shows and events a season in those days, all benefits for the community. We still have them of course, but they were larger and far more exciting—true fashion shows, because we had all of the fashion merchandise to show.

"We had an annual benefit show at The Carnegie with 2,000 in attendance. We brought in designers like Ralph Lauren, Calvin Klein, Oscar de la Renta. We had another show called Fashionlogue for 1,000 that benefitted the opera.

"We still support benefits financially and in other ways. That has not gone away. But the way we support the community is different, because attendance was going down at fashion shows. The ladies who lunch are few and far between. But that's the way it should be as we're going into the 21st century. The changes have been for the betterment of the business. You may not like it, you may balk at it, but that's what you have to deal with."

LOCAL SHOPPERS, 2006

From Annie O'Neill, "Ah, the Memories! The Clock, Tic Toc, Santa, Furs," Pittsburgh Post-Gazette, *September 4, 2006.*

A *Post-Gazette* reporter collected memories of Kaufmann's from readers as the store was re-branded as Macy's.

"As a child growing up in the Pittsburgh area, life was enjoyable. My father worked at J&L Steel in Aliquippa and his job as a steelworker and my mother's job as a school teacher provided the money to take care of a family of five. One of the places that provided the luxuries in the area was Kaufmann's, the big downtown department store full of staples and many luxurious imports. The memories included the big ornate clock at Fifth Avenue and Smithfield, and the type of atmosphere that made you want to buy something in the healthiest departments store between New York and Chicago…Who could forget the chocolate cookies from the bakery on the arcade and Santa at Christmas and the decorations and the very large crowds…It was such a rich history in the development of the city and the area and the name will be missed."—Keith from Philadelphia

"The famous saying, 'We'll meet under the Kaufmann's clock,' was forever in my vocabulary. I can remember as a child having my mother take me on a bus to meet relatives under the clock and go to the Tic Toc for lunch. As a child, this was the highlight of the day.

When Kaufmann's closed its fur department, I was first in line to purchase a fur coat, with my father's charge. How excited I was to own that coat as it came from Kaufmann's. To this day I still have that fur coat, and cherish that forever."—Lois M. Sherry, Delray Beach, FL

"Back in the early '50s, I worked for Blue Cross in the Union Trust Building and watched the daily process of adding on to the Kaufmann's Department Store from our window on the second floor. My desk was right there and we saw everything that went down the avenue, including Gen, Dwight D. Eisenhower when he was running for president.

We spent our lunch hours walking through the store. Then, of course, there was the famous clock. Everyone met someone there every day. The pass word was 'Meet you under the clock' and every one in Pittsburgh knew it was the Kaufmann's clock.

Oh, what happy memories we have of the store."—Barbara Hammond Pyles, Greer, SC

LOCAL SHOPPER, 2015

From Frank G. Coyle, "Shopping at Kaufmann's Used to Be a Grand Experience," letter to the Pittsburgh Post-Gazette, *July 19, 2015.*

My earliest recollection of Kaufmann's is as a young boy getting a suit in the men's department. It was summer and I rode the trolley Downtown by myself. Mom made sure I had the correct change and knew how to board the street car. Dad met me at Max Azen Furs, and we walked down Wood Street, took a right on Fifth and headed toward the clock.

Entering Kaufmann's we rode those rattling wooden escalators. In the men's department, a salesman met us. Dad showed me how to find the union label in the coat pocket—union suits are better quality, he explained. The tailor stood me on a platform and measured for a perfect fit. When it came time to pay, Dad pulled a slip of paper from his wallet on which was written his charge plate number. I can imagine the look I'd get from a store clerk were I to try that today. Afterward, we returned to Max Azen's, where Dad got me aboard a trolley and said to make sure I didn't miss my stop.

The years passed, I left Pittsburgh and served 25 years in the Navy. Occasionally I'd return home and visit the Big Store, by now a Macy's. Gone were the personal services and the union labels.

The economics of store mergers and closings are inevitable, but in the process cities lose their souls. I'm glad to have experienced the grandeur that made Pittsburgh unique.

KAUFMANN'S TRIVIA TIMELINE

1881—Men's suits are sold for between \$1.87 and \$17.50; Kaufmann's advertises them as the "best bargains in the world"; the store issues a fashion magazine called *Clothier*.

1884—During the spring price wars, a customer brings a competitor's ad to the store to show the same merchandise for 25 to 33 percent less and is given a free watch with the purchase.

April 24, 1888—*Pittsburgh Daily Post* notes that Kaufmann's opened a "Photograph Gallery" and offered six photos to patrons of Boys' Clothing or the Ladies Cloak Department ("no tintypes, mind you, but real artistically mounted Photographs").

1890—In December, Kaufmann's corner window features Shakespeare's "Seven Ages of Man," illustrated by seven moving wax figures.

1891—In an Easter promotion, Kaufmann's has a new fifty-dollar bill sent from Washington, D.C., in a sealed envelope and placed in a large sugar egg in its corner window. The boy who guessed the number on the bill would receive it, and those who guessed the next three closest numbers would receive ten dollars, five dollars and the sugar egg, respectively. The store gives the public a hint: the number was between 1 and 50,000. If no one guessed the actual number, the number closest to the number on the bill would receive the money. There is only one hitch: the contest is limited to those who had made a purchase in the boys' department.

1892—December store advertisements let the public know that Kaufmann's is adding a Book Department, a Candy Department and a Jewelry Department.

1901—Kaufmann's is closed for President McKinley's funeral.

1900–1908—Kaufmann's runs ads in local German newspapers, as well as in the English press.

1904—During the thirty-third anniversary sale, Kaufmann's offers to pay the cost of a round-trip train ticket for anyone living forty miles outside Pittsburgh who buys ten dollars' worth of merchandise.

1905—Kaufmann's tests a new marketing strategy: buy a pair of men's trousers and receive a metal cuspidor; in March, Kaufmann's features a "lifelike panoramic view" of the Johnstown Flood in its auditorium (there is no charge for the exhibition).

1907—Kaufmann's holds its first "One Day Sale" on Friday each week; "Stick to Kaufmann's, the Big Store, and you're bound to save money," the store advertises; during the panic, while people are losing confidence in paper money, the store ships tons of silver dollars from a western bank to pay employees and make change; on August 6, advertisements reference the "Kaufmann clock" at the corner of Fifth and Smithfield for the first time.

1909—The store distributes 125,000 pictures of Lincoln to Pittsburgh schoolchildren for the centennial of Lincoln's birth.

1913—"A pretty ankle is deserving of a jeweled anklet. Let the prudes rave all they want…One shouldn't wear rhinestones. One should wear jade or other jewels," declares model Henrietta McKenzie in an article about new fashion. Miss McKenzie, "known via the motion pictures throughout the world," is at Kaufmann's modeling new fashions, including ankle bracelets.

1915—Miss Dolly Morris of Beechview, the "Pantalette Girl," appears in Kaufmann's Fashion Play and Style Promenade as the "Girl of Today." Miss Morris is the first girl in Pittsburgh to appear in public in the new fashion.

1920—Clerks need special permission from the floor walker to hand purchases directly to customers (purchases were usually sent to the Parcel Room, where customers would pick them up before leaving the store).

1920s—The "Kaufmann Quartette," four male employees under the direction of Walter C. Steinecker, travels across the region to give free community concerts.

1929—In April, the Kaufmann Players presents *The Red Widow* at the Nixon Theater to raise money for the store's Beneficial Association.

1930—In February, Kaufmann's advertises that "every ping-pong need is readily met" for those interested in the sport, which is making a national revival ("Wholesome exercise for you if you play ping pong at home"); Kaufmann's briefly uses cartoon character "Colonel Cherrio" to advertise the store on the comic pages of local newspapers.

1930s—Kaufmann's has one hundred men and ninety-six vehicles on the road every day making store deliveries.

1932—Dick Powell, singer on Kaufmann's radio program, leaves Pittsburgh for Hollywood.

1934—Albert Einstein stays with E.J. Kaufmann during his visit to Pittsburgh.

1938—Kaufmann's sells inexpensive "utility frocks" for housewives and service workers.

1941—During the war, Kaufmann's starts a Wartime Buffet service in the restaurant during the Christmas rush. Buffet dinners are served every Monday night from 5:00 p.m. to 8:00 p.m.; in March, Kaufmann's conducts a contest to search for a local child to appear on the national *Quiz Kids* radio program. After auditions at the store, the winner would go to Chicago to represent Pittsburgh on the national broadcast. Adults could submit questions used to quiz the kids.

1946–47—Kaufmann's awards 13,591 courtesy dollars and roses to employees for courteous and efficient service during the store's seventy-fifth anniversary year.

1948—Actor James Mason and his wife visit the store so she could sign copies of her book *Del Palma* for customers.

1949—In April, Douglas Fairbanks Jr. speaks on behalf of CARE as part of the report on the Paris openings at the store; in October, Hopalong Cassidy appears at the Kaufmann's Parking Garage; Christmas windows introduce a new character called "Screechie, the Little Lost Chord," who only learned to sing when Santa found him a new home and new friends. Loudspeakers broadcast the story in front of the windows on Smithfield Street.

1951—Charlie Spivak and his orchestra entertain Kaufmann's employees at the Easter Rabbit Hop.

1955—During Christmas, Kaufmann's features a Felt Bar that sold ribbon, glitter, felt and patterns for those making their own decorations; Kaufmann's still has large millinery workrooms making and repairing hats.

1957—To address the downtown transportation problem, Kaufmann's sets up a "Courtesy Caravan" service. Those needing a ride could pick up a "C" card at store service desks and hold the card up as they stood on the streets. Drivers were asked to give them a lift; Carnegie Library moves its downtown and business libraries to the Kaufmann's Annex. It was the second Carnegie Library branch at the store; an earlier pickup window had been closed in the 1920s; Jane Russell visits the Lingerie Department, and Mrs. America greets visitors at the Steelaire "House on the Roof."

1958—During the Kaufmann's Space Show in April, Sharick, an American space dog, visits the auditorium, and a lecturer explains "Space Age Facts."

1960—Paul Anka visits the record department and signs record albums for customers.

1960s—"Mr. Zachery" appears in Kaufmann's wig salon downtown during a clinic, "Discover the Wonderful Ways of the Wig," to help customers hide their special hair problems.

1966—Not to be outdone by Santa, the Easter Bunny meets children in the Kaufmann's restaurant for a "Tiny Tot Tea Party." On the menu: Easter bunny sandwiches, molded fruit salad, Easter basket ice cream, nest of jellied eggs and lemonade; Kaufmann's advertises Dacron dresses with the line, "WOW-ZAP-POW! SEE...IT'S CHEMICAL MAN." In the store, customers could watch a DuPont musical show exploring the magic of chemistry.

1967—An Easter animal safari in Kaufmann's auditorium features rabbits, a parrot, a calf and puppies from the Animal Rescue League.

1986—At Christmas, Jingle Bell Bears, employees in bear costumes, raise $40,000 for the Make-a-Wish foundation.

1996—Painters discover a seventy-fifth-anniversary plaque presented to E.J. Kaufmann by the store's employees between walls in the subbasement. The plaque is five feet, six inches high and weighs three hundred pounds.

BIBLIOGRAPHY

The Department Store Museum. http://www.thedepartmentstoremuseum.org.

Dombrowsky, Don. "Kaufmann's Restaurant Group One of Pittsburgh's Oldest and Best-Kept Secrets." *Restaurateur of Western Pennsylvania* (March 1994): 8–9.

Dry Goods Economist. "Confident Buying" (May 1935).

Fortune 30, no. 5. "Seller's Market" (November 1944): 123–30.

Harris, Leon. *Merchant Princes: An Intimate History of Jewish Families Who Built Great Department Stores.* New York: Harper and Row, 1979.

Howard, Vicki. *From Main Street to Mall: The Rise and Fall of the American Department Store.* Philadelphia: University of Pennsylvania Press, 2015.

Kaufmann Department Store Records. MSS 373, Historical Society of Western Pennsylvania Library and Archives Division. Manuscript Boxes 1–12, *Storagram* Box, Photograph Boxes 1–10. John H. Heinz History Center, Pittsburgh, PA.

Markowitz, Jack. "Minding the Store." *Pittsburgh Tribune Review*, April 26, 1998.

Miller, Donald. "Kaufmann's Rich Legacy." *Pittsburgh Post Gazette Sunday Magazine* (November 10, 1996).

Pittsburgh Post-Gazette Archives. https://archives.post-gazette.com. Search terms like "Kaufmann's," Kaufmann's Christmas," "Kaufmann's Anniversary" and the year.

Pitz, Marylynne. "The Kaufmann Legacy." *Pittsburgh Post-Gazette.* http://newsinteractive.post-gazette.com/kaufmann.

Whittaker, Jan. *Service and Style: How the Department Store Fashioned the Middle Class.* New York: St. Martin's Press, 2006.

INDEX

ABOUT THE AUTHOR

Letitia Savage discovered downtown Kaufmann's and the McKnight branch after moving to Pittsburgh as a teenager, and her favorite Tic Toc desserts were the baked custard or a pecan ball with hot fudge. She earned a BS in biology, taught in a small private school and established environmental education programs in several Allegheny County parks before becoming an environmental consultant.

She began freelancing as a writer while in college and has contributed to local and national publications, including *Country Journal*, *Kitchen Garden*, *Dog Fancy* and *The Chronicle of the Horse*. She lives in Sewickley, Pennsylvania, with husband William Ebner. When not writing, she enjoys gardening, volunteering as an environmental educator and spending time with her horse and dog. This is her first book.